Macroeconomics and Monopoly Capitalism

Macroeconomics and Monopoly Capitalism

Ben Fine
Reader in Economics
Birkbeck College, London

Andy Murfin
Senior Economic Analyst
Henley Centre for Forecasting, London

ST. MARTIN'S PRESS   New York

All rights reserved. For information write:
St. Martin's Press, Inc., 175 Fifth Avenue, New York, NY 10010
Printed in Great Britain
First published in the United States of America in 1984

ISBN 0-312-50336-9

Library of Congress Cataloging in Publication Data

Fine, Ben.
Macroeconomics and monopoly capitalism.

Bibliography: p.
Includes index.
1. Capitalism.   2. Macroeconomics.
3. Economics.   I. Murfin, Andy.   II. Title.
HB501.F49 1984   330.12′2   84-16034
ISBN 0-312-50336-9

Contents

1 Postwar Capitalism and Economic Theory

I INTRODUCTION

The postwar boom of the advanced capitalist countries allowed the Keynesian revolution to prosper in the realm of academic economics just as the collapse of that boom has been conducive to the resurgence of the monetarist counter-revolution. It is the argument of this book that both of these schools of thought have maintained a vast distance between their core concepts and the economic realities of the postwar period. The range of phenomena encompassed by standard macroeconomics, whether Keynesian or monetarist, is both narrow and, to a large extent, wide of the mark in identifying the crucial determinants of economic growth. Essentially, macroeconomics is concerned with expenditure-related categories alone, and the production of commodities leads a shadowy existence in the underworld of microeconomics where assumptions are made of exogenous production functions and consumer preferences and the absence of externalities and economies of scale. It is both the neglect of microeconomics and the particular content that it has encompassed which has allowed macroeconomics to be the pearl of the discipline of economics. Whilst fundamental changes, such as monopolisation and state industrial intervention, have been generalised at the micro level of the economy, microeconomics has tended to ignore these except as a partial equilibrium application of conventional theory. This has enabled macroeconomics to follow suit and pretend that it has captured the essential economic relations which constitute modern capitalism through exchange-based macroeconomic aggregates.

The resulting myths and misconceptions surrounding the explanatory power of Keynesianism and monetarism are exposed in the following two chapters. Subsequently, we turn our attention to the representatives of the Kaleckian school, or Post-Keynesians. There are differences between the writers within this school, but these are less significant than the assumptions and approach that they share in common. Reynolds (1981) explores these differences, but we will draw attention to them only in passing. What this school has attempted to do is to locate the macroeconomy relative to generalised microeconomic relations, most notably in an emphasis on the role played by monopolisation. In our view, this represents progress over traditional macroeconomics since it attempts to address a significant part of economic reality that is otherwise put aside. However, this school remains too attached to much of the conventional framework of analysis by continuing to focus on exchange relations, occasionally supplemented by distributional considerations. It is a departure from, but not a break with, conventional macroeconomics since it gives attention to conditions, such as monopolisation, that violate the presumptions of the orthodoxy, whilst remaining committed to the determining role of aggregate demand, for example.

To a large extent, the book is negative in the sense of being critical without offering an alternative. But this is too one-sided a view of criticism. Our critical analysis of Keynesianism, monetarism and the Kaleckian school allows us to expose what is absent from their theory. In the following section, we refer to what are major aspects of modern capitalism, and these correspond in many respects to what has been excluded by these three schools of thought. Our exercise is positive in that it reveals that conventional ways of thinking have distanced economics from the economy. In the course of doing this we expose for consideration alternative objects of analysis and ways of proceeding. This creates a task for economics but it is one that has not been pursued in depth in this book since its motive is more to persuade the reader of its importance. Whilst our own approach to an assessment of economics and the economy is informed by Marxist political economy, our intention has not been to justify this nor to convert the reader to our way of thinking. Rather our intention has been far more modest: to attempt to convince economists of the need to broach new problems and correspondingly to break with conventional theory. Essentially our focus would be upon industrial organisation and reorganisation with factors such as technical innovation, scale economies and monopolisation being considered as pervasive and central. In our final chapter we confess to being sanguine about our chances of success in persuading economics to take a new direction, since economics has exhibited a remarkable ability to thrive whilst distancing itself from economic realities. Hopefully, this book will contribute to and offer encouragement to those whose economics is not to remain academic.

II MODERN CAPITALISM

Two features are crucial in understanding the character of contemporary capitalism. One is the internationalisation of capital, most notably through multinational corporations and as reflected in the interpenetration within the advanced capitalist countries of trade, finance and investment. The other is state economic intervention. The extent and directions of this state economic intervention in the western capitalist economies are widely known. Its composition and its size however differ vastly from what might be envisaged within strict Keynesian principles. Keynesian activism would not seem to require that the government regulate upwards of 40% or 50% of output and yet, while this situation has evolved, the role of the government has still been conventionally analysed in Keynesian terms. The political role of the state and the nature of its intervention are beyond Keynesian comprehension, apart from their effects on government financing requirements. The state's role in influencing aggregate demand is obviously important, but it is a misconception to view this as the essence of state activity.

Keynesian theory and policy-making is predominantly concerned with capitalist relations of exchange. The grounds it gives for state intervention to reduce unemployment are based on the failure of the market mechanism to provide full employment. Its policy prescriptions concern the effect of policy on the overall level of demand as well as on the distribution of expenditure between the state and the private sector. The differences in policy prescription between Keynesians and monetarists lie in the empirical differences within the operations of markets, although the underlying conception of the economy is shared. For our purposes, the central factor in need of emphasis is that state policy-making has not always been organised around Keynesian methods of regulation. In many countries various forms of economic planning and industrial policy have been the basis of state intervention. Hesselman (1983) documents the trends in European industrial intervention and shows them to be wide-ranging, even under allegedly non-interventionist governments. This is not to say that industrial policies in the UK, for example, have been either coherent (or comprehensible) but that even in the UK intervention is so extensive as to render meaningless any suggestion that the Thatcher Government is in any sense taking the economy "towards laissez-faire". While proclaiming itself to be anti-interventionist, it is effectively highly interventionist. The implication of the above discussion is that the forces behind and the results of state economic intervention cannot be summarised by the aggregate categories of Keynesian theory. Similarly, Keynesianism is but one (arguably minor) component of the state's regulation of the economy. (This form of regulation is discussed in its cyclical context below).

It is the interaction of state economic intervention and the internationalisation of capital which explain the unprecedented stimulus to the growth of world trade, investment and finance. During the twentieth century there have been fundamental changes in the extent, direction and origin of international firms. This reflects the breaking down of old economic empires as spheres for trade and investment as the interpenetration of trade and investment within the advanced capitalist economies has proceeded. This development has been characterised by its unevenness, both within and between countries (again something which conventional analysis would not perceive because of its preoccupation with the proportionate growth of existing economic activity and its focus upon the short run).

At the heart of the internationalisation and interpenetration of capital has been its concentration into a complex system of multinational corporations (MNCs). There are over 10,000 MNCs with almost ten times as many foreign affiliates (United Nations: 1983B). These aggregate figures conceal the great variety of size both of parent MNCs and of their offspring. In 1978, for example, some 430 of the world's largest MNCs accounted for three quarters of overseas affiliates and direct investment (Dunning, Haberich and Stopford: 1981). Relatively small numbers of firms dominate the economy when looked at sector by sector, as is illustrated by the evidence for industrial concentration given by Dunning and Pearce (1981), and by our discussion below of the oil and car industries.

Behind this increasing concentration of world capital emerges a pattern of international rivalry and uneven development. In particular, these reflect the secular decline of the US and UK domestic economies against the advances made by Japan and West Germany. Within this evolution, however, is a complexity of developments concerning the nature of US hegemony. The treatment of multinationals within the conventional literature fails to encompass this pervasive influence of internationally organised capital over production, trading and finance, and over the changing international division of labour. Instead, such responses and movements are subsumed within analyses such as the aptly named "eclectic theory" of international firms' operations; see Dunning (1979), for example.

In this theory, firms from a particular country must either have specific *ownership* advantages over the firms of other countries, or these other countries must have *locational* advantages over the home country if the firm is to choose to operate there. The third factor governing multinational operation in the "eclectic theory" is the costs associated with market imperfections, such as for patenting and licensing or the use of market power.

This approach provides a theory of trade (possibly internal to the firm) in comparative advantages plus a theory of market imperfections in the tradition of conventional microeconomics. The role of the state in determining national accumulation conditions is just another factor entering into the calculation of relative advantage. As with much conventional analysis, the concept of the multinational firm is analysed solely in terms of its implied deviation from a (non-existent) idea of perfect market economy. That is, it offers no explanation of the phenomenon of internationalisation at all, except on the basis of given locational, firm or market advantages. (See Sugden (1983) for a critical appraisal of the conventional theory of the multinational enterprise). So whilst attention has been paid by economics both to MNCs and to state intervention beyond macroeconomic demand management, such attention has not brought about a reassessment (and downgrading) of the significance of the latter.

III THE POSTWAR BOOM

As much attention should be paid to unevenness as to the uniformity of growth in the postwar boom. This is illustrated by the differences in growth rates which have been moderated to some extent following the crisis of the 1970s. Whilst differences in growth rates appear to reflect country characteristics, they also correspond to different balances in domestic and international expansion. Significantly, the US and UK have experienced the lowest domestic rates of growth while more fully internationalising production, whilst Japan and West Germany have witnessed the highest domestic growth rates as the basis on which to expand exports. We do not propose a simple crowding-out theory connecting

Annual Average Growth Rates of Manufacturing Output

	1955–73	1973–82
UK	3.1	0.3
USA	4.7	1.9
West Germany	6.0	1.8
France	6.2	2.2
Italy	7.3	2.1
Japan	13.8	3.7

domestic and foreign production, but the evidence is suggestive of reorganisation of firms (and hence the economy) through international production or upon a domestic basis, although these are not necessarily mutually exclusive. It is through such domestic and international reorganisation of production, aided and abetted by state intervention in industry and welfare, that the postwar economy prospered, albeit unevenly.

In this light, it is possible to understand cyclical movements around trend growth rates during the postwar boom as domestic economies were reorganised and integrated into the world economy. These cyclical movements, however, became increasingly synchronised as the interpenetration of economies and concentration of capital proceeded. There is now a global recession and a requirement for a major restructuring of capital so that even large, internationally organised firms such as Chrysler face profound difficulties. It is our contention that these cyclical movements cannot be understood within the framework of conventional macroeconomic analysis. Such analysis tends to obscure the sources of growth by focusing on exchange management alone. Growth is seen as the unexplained trend around which there are fluctuations. By contrast, it is the forces behind the creation of that trend through industrial reorganisation which is equally the source of fluctuations, and it is the limits upon that reorganisation, whether in the domestic or international plane, that have brought the postwar boom to a halt.

The misconceptions surrounding the role of state economic intervention and the internationalisation of capital are also reflected in the treatment of the US' role in the long boom. For example, the establishment of world monetary arrangements at Bretton Woods in 1944 is often regarded solely as the beginning of an efficient means of organising world trade and payments. However, we would argue that this institution is best seen as a method by which the US was able to establish world hegemony (see also Gamble and Walton: 1976). The dollar for a long time was effectively "as good as gold", while as postwar reconstruction proceeded the US lent dollars, via such methods as Marshall Aid, to enable other economies to purchase US goods. Further, while these conditions correspond to particular institutional arrangements apparently concerned with exchange phenomena, their operation held implications for the role of the state and the position of capital in debtor countries. The restrictions tied to these financial arrangements were a lever by which the US could control and organise economic activity on a global basis. Much of the same is at present emerging from the operations of the IMF. Thus while at first sight these institutions deal only with macromanagement, potentially they have as important an effect on planning arrangements and the restructuring of capital in the economies concerned.

IV STAGNATION

With the onset of stagnation coupled with rampant inflation in the 1970s, conventional economic analysis has responded essentially by introducing expectations into existing models. This is taken up in Chapters 2 and 3. Some economists, however, have attempted to reconcile economics with economic reality and it is this Post-Keynesian school that we examine critically in the second part of the book. Associated with their ideas about the capitalist economy is the central role played by stagnation and economic realities such as monopolisation. As an introduction to some of the themes taken up later, we examine here briefly the nature of monopolisation in two industries—oil and automotive—and what might be implied for them by theories of stagnation.

The survival of the oil industry effectively depends upon monopolisation. The fixed costs of development are the main cost components; once established the running costs are very low. If revenues are to cover fixed costs, operators will have an incentive to sell all that they can; this would lead to a problem of chronic excess capacity and tend to lower price. It can be argued (see Fine and Harris: 1984) that the organising force behind the world oil industry is the need to maintain profitable oil production in the USA. There has been a conflict between groupings of the US producers, and a division between the US market and the rest of the world, with declining collusion amongst producers over the postwar period.

Since 1945, the US has used its economic-political hegemony to increase its share of Middle East oil reserves, which were inexpensive. In the US there was a problem of rising production costs. As a result of these factors, the "oil crisis" of the early 1970s can be interpreted as the discovery of a solution both to the erosion of the world cartel of the major oil companies, and to the pressures on domestic US production. The oil price hike has restored the profitability of US producers and has guaranteed revenues sufficient to unite the major and non-major companies in a cartel. The ability of the OPEC countries to appropriate some of these revenues is a result, and not a cause, of the oil price rise.

Thus, the cartelisation of the oil industry can be viewed as one product of postwar US hegemony. In the stagnationist theory of those such as Kalecki and Cowling, such monopolisation is associated with a restriction of output as monopoly profits are sought. This raises the problem of identifying whether output is restricted. From a crude empirical basis we argue that the oil cartel has engineered a steady growth of oil production rather than a cutback and move to stagnation. Blair (1977) shows how exactly the major oil companies have been able to control oil supply up to 1972. Individual countries' supplies have fluctuated enormously, but the sum for the top nine countries is a simple growth path which must have been determined by collusion.

This raises doubts concerning the restrictive nature of monopolisation. The world automotive industry is also highly monopolised; in 1980 the top eight firms accounted for 74.7% of total production (and the top four for 51%) (UN: 1983A, and see also Murfin: 1982). Despite the extent of monopolisation and the evidence that the industry faces pervasive excess capacity, output has continued to expand considerably over the past decade. In 1970 output was 29.6 m cars, 33.3 m in 1975 and 38.2 m by 1981 (UN: 1983A). Again, while there have been changes in the national components of the total (such as the run-down of the UK as a production base), reflecting the changing international division of labour and restructuring of the industry in the face of changing economies of scale, the total again exhibits an expansionary growth path. Thus, we question here the very idea that monopolisation either leads to a restriction of output or to a general stagnationary tendency. A more direct attack on stagnation theory is undertaken in part two of this book.

V SUMMARY

In this chapter we have raised questions concerning the conventional economic analyses associated with Keynesianism, Monetarism and Kalecki. The purpose of this book is to broaden the attack to show both the underlying inconsistencies of conventional theory and its inappropriateness as a foundation for examining the present stage of capitalism. Our intention is to emphasise those factors we believe to be crucial to an understanding of modern capitalism—factors which are not as yet placed at the centre of economic analysis. The lack of consideration within macroeconomics given to state economic intervention, most notably in the form of industrial policy, and to the dominance of multinational corporations, is a legacy of Keynesianism. Macro-policy receives priority over industrial policy within economic theory, a priority which is even maintained within the Kaleckian approach, where facets of industry are at least considered in terms of the effect of monopoly. In subsequent chapters we hope to demonstrate the failure of economics to deal with the economy, a failure which will require a radical revision of economic analysis if it is to make any progress towards realism.

PART I

Introduction

In this part, we examine conventional macroeconomic theory. In recent years, this has been dominated by the debate between Keynesianism and monetarism. We devote a chapter to each of these. We attempt to give a fair presentation of the two schools of thought. By doing so, it is possible to see that they have more in common than might be supposed from the exaggerated differences that dominate their conflicts. At the same time, our account of macroeconomics allows us to expose its limitations in two different but related ways. First, the concepts employed are shown in many respects to be deficient even on their own terms. Secondly, as the world economy has moved into a crisis of growth, the divorce between the concepts of macroeconomics and the economy it attempts to explain (and control) has widened. This in turn throws into doubt the supposed validity of macroeconomics for the period of the postwar boom, when it could claim (falsely) some major responsibility for it.

2 The Myths of Keynesianism

INTRODUCTION

In the postwar period economic theory has not been exclusively dominated by Keynesianism. Orthodox teaching and research in economics have continued to rely upon the principles laid down more than a hundred years ago by the marginalist revolution. But they do so predominantly in the area of microeconomics which has survived not so much through the introduction of new ideas as through the presentation of the old ones in the form of increasingly difficult mathematics. Orthodox economics has advanced very little but has made a great effort to change its appearance. This has had the effect of consolidating the separation of this branch of economics from the realm of popular ideas, a separation that is perhaps fundamentally dependent on the rarified assumptions upon which the theory is built. So abstracted are the foundations of microeconomic theory that they are certain to test the patience of both the independent thinker and the independent businessman.

By contrast, Keynesianism has reigned supreme not only in the kingdom of intellectuals but also in the realm of popular ideas. Whilst macroeconomics has not escaped a mathematical, nor rigorous, treatment as its exponents would describe it, it has remained amenable to an understanding much wider than is encompassed by those holding the necessary technical skills. Accordingly, a "conventional wisdom", which is shared by economists and non-economists alike, has been built up around Keynesianism and around the position of Keynes himself.

THE "CONVENTIONAL WISDOM"

The first component of this wisdom suggests that the Keynesian revolution received a significant stimulus from the unemployment of the 1930s. Taken in historical perspective, and not in isolation from other factors, this is an extremely inadequate view. Since unemployment, even if not on the scale of the 1930s, had been a pressing economic problem before, not least in the 1920s in Britain, a novel theoretical response to it cannot be explained by the existence of the problem of unemployment alone.

This leads to the second element of the conventional wisdom, one which focuses on the individual genius of Keynes. He made theoretical innovations which both explained persistent unemployment and proposed a variety of potential remedies. In doing so, it is believed that a break was made with existing economic theory—classical economics, as Keynes termed it. By rejecting Say's Law which denied the possibility of the generalised excess supply of commodities, the notion of ineffective demand (and involuntary unemployment) could be introduced as the conceptual hallmark of the Keynesian revolution and as the target of economic policy. Ineffective demand was to be reduced subject to satisfactory price level stability.

The problem of relying on the intellectual genius of Keynes to explain the Keynesian revolution is that the principal ideas involved were not new even to Keynes himself. He had argued most eloquently for reflationary policies in the 1920s. Conceptually, he identified Malthus as an intellectual precursor because of the latter's emphasis on the role of landlords in creating demand through the expenditure of their rental revenue. To use the genius of Keynes to explain the Keynesian revolution tends to make a false analogy with progress in the physical sciences. In these, although this parable can be equally misleading, individuals can make conceptual or experimental discoveries that are rapidly disseminated. In economics, ideas tend to be around for a long time before they constitute a new school of thought. Consequently, the explanation of a revolution in economic thought has to focus upon the acceptance rather than the generation of new ideas over a very lengthy period of time. By way of digression, it can be observed that this creates major problems for the Kuhnian concept of paradigm shift, when applied to economics, whatever its validity for the physical sciences. Economics also tends to be dominated by the Anglo-Saxon world and word. Those "foreign" econo- mists who have made an impact have been obliged to find their way into the English-speaking journals. It is far from clear that the weight of ideas has been the motive force behind Keynesian or other revolutions in economic thought. This is confirmed when examining the international spread of ideas. Precursors of Keynesian ideas are to be found in theory and in practice in Germany, for example, although their association with Nazism has also served to obscure their existence (see Backhaus: 1983).

However, Keynes could still be considered to have played the major role in revolutionising economic thinking because of his powers of persuasion in gaining the acceptance of new ideas. Undoubtedly Keynes increasingly became a prominent figure in the making of both economic policy and thinking until his death in 1946. This raises the question of whether Keynes was leading the wave of new ideas or whether he was being carried along by it at its head. A historical parallel with some irony will help to illustrate the point. Winston Churchill, against whose economic policies in the 1920s Keynes directed his most vehement criticism, became Prime Minister during the war because of his earlier stand, un- popular with his colleagues, against German militarism. The victory of the Allies is easily credited to the warleaders and this idea is encouraged during and after the war for propa- ganda and political purposes. Unfortunately for Churchill, this proved of little consequence in the immediate postwar election which swept the Labour Party to power.

Clearly Churchill had not caused the war by standing out against Germany nor had he won the war, although, if an individual were to be identified with the winning of the war, it would probably be Churchill (leaving aside much neglected Russian claims). Similarly, it is easy to see why Keynes should have come to have had his name identified with the revolution in economic thought because of his intellectual and policy influence. But the more this is examined in isola- tion, the more it tends to obscure the real origins and causes of the Keynesian revolution, just as a biography of Churchill would fail to explain the cause and course of the second world war.

At a more specific level, Keynes as the cause rather than as the figurehead of changing theory and policy is highly questionable. There was no Keynes-inspired intervention in Britain in the 1930s, whilst in the United States Keynesian policies were adopted in the form of the New Deal without the necessity of Keynes' influence (see, for example, Mattick: 1978). The massive government expenditure in the war was hardly a response to Keynes' ideas and influences. Although the first budget on Keynesian lines was prepared in 1941, this was in the context of substantial economic planning and controls that could be assessed in aggregate for their effect on demand, but which, individually and collectively, far exceeded the prescriptions of Keynesianism in pursuit of the war effort. Following the war, Keynes' immediate influence was brought to an end by his death in 1946, a demise precipitated by hard work in his relatively unsuccessful negotiations for Britain with America over postwar international monetary relations. During the war, the commitment to full employment and more general economic and social management received its stimulus from the aspirations of working people whose cooperation was essential for the successful conduct of the war. Whilst, as observed, the economic form in which these policies were to be framed owed much to Keynes' influence, what remains questionable is that their very formulation is due to him. The pressure for Keynesian policies, in Britain as elsewhere, owes most to changing political circumstances, ones which saw the emergence of political parties able to assume power and pursue the policies of social reformism as the means of representing the interests of labour. The growth of political parties representing labour in this way was not accidental, nor a simple response to the harsh conditions suffered in the 1930s. The preceding years had witnessed an increasing concentration of production under capitalism. This in turn had stimulated the growth of trade unions with a degree of economic strength that sought, in one form or another, a means of political representation. State economic intervention was inevitable and increasing in significance during the interwar period. Its relative maturity in the postwar period under the conceptual guise of Keynesianism should not mislead us into believing that this theory is the root of increasing state economic management.

This in turn leads us to reject a third component of the conventional wisdom surrounding Keynesianism. It is that the theory and practice of Keynesianism is a major factor explaining the postwar boom. Certainly, a major difference in this period has been the extension of state economic intervention, and this has been crucial in stimulating the unprecedented growth experienced after the war. But it is a Keynesian ideology and mythology that explains and identifies that intervention with macroeconomic management. Both in extent and in variety, state economic intervention has far surpassed the needs dictated by Keynesian theory and this brings into question the causative significance of Keynesianism as economic policy. Essentially, Keynesian theory demands that the economy be analysed in terms of the levels of expenditure generated through the application of fiscal and monetary policy. In doing so, it renders itself more or less oblivious to the details of the direction of these expenditures, which would be thought of as lying at a lower level of microeconomic policy or as involving distributive or welfare considerations. Consequently, Keynesianism is unable to explain the massive increase in state expenditure. On the other hand, it is almost certain to congratulate itself for periods of successful growth. Since demand will be high in such conditions, whether it plays a causative role or not, successful growth will be simply read off as successful manipulation of demand. To disagree necessarily involves the view that growth is caused by something else. Significantly, this is the perspective adopted by monetarism as the modern economic ideology of laissez-faire. In this it is argued that the postwar boom occurred despite the adoption of Keynesian policies.

Our view is rather different. It sees macroeconomic policy as one among many forms taken by the state in its economic interventions. These interventions have been significant in promoting the accumulation of capital but manipulation of the conditions of demand are by no means the most important factor. The state has been actively involved in policies for reorganising industry as well as in providing social conditions conducive to growth (such as the welfare state).

In this perspective, it can be recognised that the growth process is not liable to be smooth. Both the reorganisation of industry and the development of the social conditions in which it accumulates are not reducible to the provision of appropriate levels of demand as suggested by Keynesian theory. Nor are these considerations to be relegated to microeconomic implementation within a grand overall macroeconomic policy. Whilst such a view may carry some conviction in the context of any single policy, it does not do so when industry and welfare are considered as a whole. Indeed, it is more appropriate to reverse the causal relationship between macroeconomic policy and industrial and welfare policy. The postwar boom has fed upon state industrial and welfare provision to bring about economic and social reorganisation. The rhythm of the associated growth process has been facilitated and tempered by macroeconomic policy, but such policy has not been the prime source of growth. Rather macroeconomic policy has had a very complex relationship with the underlying causes of growth. To see this, it is best to begin by examining how such policy-making has perceived itself.

It has been based on the presumption that "full employment" and other objectives of macroeconomic policy can be achieved through appropriate fiscal and monetary measures. In this perspective, economic conditions and the effect of policy on them are judged exclusively in terms of the categories of exchange, and particularly in terms of the level of aggregate demand. Consequently, the causes, symptoms and treatment of growth are all seen in terms of Keynesian categories. If, as we would argue, the causes of growth lie elsewhere, tend to generate a cyclical rhythm, and are of necessity incapable of being associated with full employment, then macroeconomic policy tends to assume almost an anarchic character, the economic equivalent of lobotomy. For the obstacles, say, to continuing growth will present symptoms to the Keynesian policy-maker who will treat these symptoms as causes. The symptoms will then be acted upon in a fashion that may or may not be conducive to overcoming the fundamental obstacles to growth. For example, the rhythm of accumulation may require a downturn. The theory of Keynesian policy may or may not accept this depending on the significance given to unemployment as opposed to inflation. Either way, the policies actually adopted may yield the opposite of the intended effect: even when resulting in "right" policy only doing so out of the combination of the two "wrongs" in diagnosis and treatment. This account explains in simplistic and unidimensional terms why policy-makers have been able to adopt deflationary and reflationary policies at the appropriate time, since the symptoms of crisis are usually unmistakable. Equally, it explains why inappropriate policies can also have been adopted in the false belief that full employment could be permanently attained. Here, however, our prime purpose is not to examine this policy-making in practice but to locate its theoretical origins. These are the failure of Keynesianism to look beyond the conditions of exchange (demand) to explain the workings of the capitalist economy.

This explains why the stagflation of the 1970s has thrown macroeconomics into disarray—other than to stimulate a revival of monetarism. The Keynesian system essentially depends on an inverse relationship between unemployment and inflation. The empirical shocks of the 1970s have totally undermined this simple relationship, which had evolved within the complacency of the Keynesian era. This is but one example of the lack of thought characteristic of the adoption of the Keynesian orthodoxy since the war:

it is not evident that the *General Theory* significantly affected the way the world thinks about economic problems. The economics profession responded to the General Theory by restating the old theory but recasting it in new Keynesian terminology.

(Rotheim (1981) p. 568)

This complacency effectively continues today despite the monetarist "counter-revolution" in macroeconomics in the 1970s and 1980s. The response to the 1970s' shocks has merely entailed the adoption of a simple and effective theoretical device. This involves the use of expectations. Essentially, anything that was explained before in macroeconomics can now be explained together with inflation by adding the price-increasing effect of self-fulfilling expectations about those prices. This represents an extraordinary conservatism on the part of macroeconomics in its response to the dramatic changes in the economy. First, these changes are merely seen in quantitative terms, of higher levels of inflation at higher levels of unemployment. Second, a new explanatory variable, expectations, suffices to chart these changed quantitative relations. Third, macroeconomics as an academic discipline is given a new lease of life as the role of expectations is integrated into pre-existing models. Finally, and most importantly, the policy perspectives generated by the expect-ations-supplemented macroeconomics remain unaltered whilst its prospects become more pessimistic as it is not only the economy but also expectations that have to be managed. We return to these issues in the following chapter.

Against this background we can examine the mythology of revolution in economic thought surrounding Keynesianism. It is necessary to do so with some caution since recently controversy has developed over the correct interpretation of Keynes. This has involved the rejection, from different points of view, of the neoclassical synthesis or IS/LM framework which was originally the Keynesian orthodoxy following Keynes' death. We leave these disputes aside for the moment and concentrate on the policy implications of Keynes' own contribution. Most significantly Keynes saw the economic problem in terms of deficient demand. Consequently, since the perception of the problem determined the nature of the solution, Keynes sought methods to regulate the overall level of demand to guarantee full employment and other features of macroeconomic stability. By doing so, he set aside the problems of the nature and direction of state economic inter-vention in general, factors that we have considered to be crucial in the postwar expansion. Certainly the Keynesian revolution had the effect of placing a focus upon the short-run level of economic activity and the state's responsibility for it. At the same time it contrived to locate the question of industrial policy at the level of microeconomics. Get the macroeconomics right and the microeconomics will look after itself (or at least will be able to be looked after).

Of course, the semantic distinction between macro- and microeconomics makes this view seem common sense. Nor do we suggest a reversal of the order of care between the two, counterposing Keynes' "penny wise, pound foolish" with an exhortation to look after the pennies so that the pounds look after themselves, where pennies serve for micro and pounds for macro. Rather it is necessary to challenge the view that the macroeconomy is constituted in Keynesian terms of aggregate demand relative to which industrial policy, or whatever, is constituted as a subordinate microeconomics. Significantly, the interwar period exhibited not only massive unemployment, but also major changes in the structural and sectoral composition of industry. Are the latter merely a subordinate factor in the working of the economic system as a whole?

That they were so for Keynes, because of his preoccupation with aggregate demand, is well illustrated by the sort of examples he used. In conditions of unemployment, the state could be well advised to employ one set of labourers to dig holes and others to fill them in. It could be even better if money were buried at the bottom of these holes. By this means it could be dug up again providing further effective demand and a reflationary increase in the money supply! By this policy the knock-on effect of the multiplier could be engaged. The important point is that the example depends upon a completely neutral industrial policy by the state. The net effect on industry as on the ground is zero except through the provision of effective demand. No doubt Keynes employs such examples to ram home his point; that completely worthless activity is beneficial to an economy if it generates effective demand. The activity need not be worthless, it could equally be a public work or an industrial venture or its support. Crucially, however, this is irrelevant to the policy (and theoretical) point that Keynes wishes to make. He is unconcerned with industrial policy and this is why he can treat it in such a cavalier way.

Whatever then the correct way to interpret Keynes' contribution to the Keynesian revolution, it is one which is consistent with little emphasis being placed on industrial policy. This is borne out by considering other aspects of the "classical economics" that were unchallenged by Keynes and which have subsequently tended to remain confined to the realms of microeconomics. Specifically, the Keynesian revolution has been silent over the question of economies of scale and externalities, the pervasive and patent presence of which are a major technical factor explaining state economic intervention. Associated with this, the competitive structure of industry is a factor that has appeared irrelevant to the Keynesian revolution. These observations apply equally to Keynes and to his interpreters. That these considerations are irrelevant to the theoretical contribution made by Keynesianism only serves to confirm the priority it gives to issues of macroeconomic management relative to which other factors are subordinate. In Keynes' own style, we might regret that macroeconomics took up its thread of development from the problems of aggregate demand rather than from those of imperfect, monopolistic competition with economies of scale. That this need not have been so—at least conceptually—is evidenced by the interwar contributions of Sraffa (1926), Chamberlin (1933) and Robinson (1933). These contributions have usually been praised as a symbolic concession to their importance so that they might be more readily passed over and forgotten.

What then was Keynes' own contribution and to what extent has it been incorporated in the Keynesian revolution? Certainly the neoclassical synthesis concedes very little to Keynes in incorporating his ideas.

KEYNES' INNOVATIONS AND THE NEOCLASSICAL SYNTHESIS

It is by now not uncommon to argue that the "neoclassical synthesis", which emerged in the postwar period, is incapable of incorporating the essential ideas of Keynes' original revolution (see Leijonhufvud (1968), Clower (1965), Morgan (1978) and from a different point of view Fine (1979) and Harris (1983)). This synthesis is a particular interpretation of

Keynesian theory in which Keynesian features, notably price inflexibility and involuntary unemployment, appear only as special empirically-determined cases of the neoclassical approach. The Keynesian model is thus not general. The development of this synthesis grew out of the popularisation of Keynes' ideas by Hicks (1937) and Hansen (1953), and later in the work of Patinkin (1965). Before we consider the components of the synthesis, we shall first briefly lay out some of the presumed vital elements of Keynes' revolution.

In terms of the pre-existing orthodoxy of economic thought in the 1930s, Keynes' radical contribution centred on his concepts of unemployment, of money and of the rate of interest. For Robinson (1973), the climate at that time for both economic policy and theory was one of general faith in laissez-faire. The principles underlying the behaviour of markets were the natural equilibrating tendency of supply and demand and the adherence to Say's Law, in which supply creates its own demand. Keynes thus rejected both classical and marginal economists in tandem on the grounds of this adherence and its inability to embrace the concept of effective demand. Within this ruling orthodoxy, monetary theory was also extremely primitive. Essentially, it was an orthodoxy governed by the neutrality of money and therefore dominated by the quantity theory.

This twinning of simple monetary theory with the adoption of Say's Law was at least internally consistent, as well as being consistent with the neglect of the timing in which economic transactions and activity take place. Say's Law of markets is grounded on the principle that whenever an individual plans a demand for a commodity, simultaneously a plan must be made to undertake to supply another commodity of equivalent value. Thus, for each individual, planned, or notional, demand will equal planned (notional) supply. If this were not the case, the rational basis on which individuals plan to balance their payments and their receipts would be destroyed. Thus, whatever the set of prices established between individuals' planned transactions, individuals must plan to equilibrate their own sales and purchases. This equilibration must also hold at the economy level so that aggregate planned supply equals aggregate planned demand.

For these plans to make the appropriate impact on the actual market, then effective as well as notional demands and supplies must be considered. Again the sum of excess demands, or supplies, must be zero but there may be some mismatching: excess demand in some markets may correspond to excess supplies in others. So in the 1930s, Keynes saw massive unemployment while the existing orthodoxy insisted there could be no generalised excess supply. In this orthodoxy, disequilibrium can only take the form of excess supplies in some markets, balanced by excess demands in other. Thus a principal aim of Keynes was to attack the prevalent view of an equilibrating economy in which nothing could be done to eradicate unemployment other than to ensure price (particularly wage) flexibility. An attack on Say's Law was a means of challenging existing views of a contemporary problem. (See Harris (1981) for further discussion).

Keynes' intention here was presumably to demonstrate that full-employment equilibrium is not the general case for the capitalist economy. Within the orthodox model, a system of excess supplies and demands emerges and this stimulates changes in prices which in turn prompt revisions to demands and supplies. Supply and demand interact such that "quantities respond to prices" i.e. individuals make quantity changes in response to given price changes. For Keynes, however, as has been made clear by the "reappraisal" initiated by Leijonhufvud (1968) and Clower (1965), there was also the likelihood of "quantities responding to quantities". Say's Law says that each supply is also a demand, for both notional and effective transactions. However, while in any particular transaction supply and demand are necessarily realised simultaneously, for each individual, the acts of supply and demand are separated in real time and space. A good example of how this can generate "quantity-quantity" responses is given by Harris (1983) in his discussion of the Keynesian consumption function. This departs from neoclassicism in making consumption depend on a quantity constraint, in the form of actual income, rather than just relative prices. Within a Walrasian general equilibrium system such a specification would not be possible, since labour supply would be simultaneous with decisions on consumption. In the orthodox modelling, the fictitious Walrasian auctioneer would ensure equilibrium trading, but in the Keynesian world, trading may occur in disequilibrium. Thus, within the consumption function is incorporated the idea that workers may be unable to sell a desired amount of their labour at a currently too high real wage and thus their consumption will be constrained by their level of income.

In this instance, there is, notionally, an excess supply of labour and an excess demand for goods. However, there is no reason why these imbalances should be felt on the market. Thus we arrive at the concept of involuntary unemployment corresponding to ineffective demand. Involuntary unemployment refers specifically to a situation where both the supply of and demand for labour would be greater than the existing level of employment (even if the real wage were to fall). This essentially requires a rise in effective demand. In our consumption function example, this would require workers being able to signal to employers their higher demand for goods consequent upon a higher level of employment. Thus, through the rejection of Say's Law, Keynes was able to introduce the concepts of involuntary unemployment and ineffective demand, with their obvious consequences across the economy, (see Fine: 1979).

Thus far, while we have admitted the sequencing of transactions through time, little has been said of the role of money, or of Keynes' theory of money and interest. If an economy is in Keynesian unemployment equilibrium, then it is not simply commodities which will be in imbalance but also money markets. Money may obviously be held as a stock or spent, be it on consumption or investment. Keynes' contribution to monetary theory emphasised the roles of uncertainty and speculation. Money will be held for speculative purposes if it is anticipated that commodities, which could be bought now, can be bought more cheaply in the future. Expectations then play a central role in monetary theory since speculative demand will depend on expectations regarding future prices. For Keynes, this was intertwined with the rate of interest, both as the cost of holding/borrowing money, and as the inverse of the price of a bond (which guarantees a fixed annual payment). As the price of bonds falls, the rate of interest rises and the demand for bonds rises. However, if the expected price of bonds falls, the expected rate of interest rises, and present demand for bonds falls. Agents will hold money and buy bonds at a future date (if their expectations are fulfilled). Thus an increase in the expected rate of interest leads to liquidity preference. This liquidity preference will also exert an impact on effective demand once the financial and commodity markets are linked. This is achieved through consideration of physical investment demand. Capitalists will invest now only if their "marginal efficiency of capital" (i.e. "that rate of discount which would make the present value of the ... returns expected from (a) capital good ... just equal to its supply price" (Keynes (1936) p. 135, see also Morgan (1978), Junankar (1972) for example), is higher than the rate of interest. This MEC necessarily includes not just the technical factors governing productions, but also the expected level of realisation, or the expected effective demand for products. Thus increased pessimism regarding the future may generate both an increase in the expected rate of interest and a fall in the MEC (since potentially profitable production possibilities are dampened by expected ineffective demand). It is possible for MEC to equal the rate of interest, and yet for the economy to be below full employment. Such a state can also be sustained by the revision of interest-rate expectations to the present interest rate. Money and uncertainty can operate to heighten the Keynesian unemployment equilibrium. Money is not a neutral veil on the economy.

Thus we have identified some of the essentially Keynesian features of the capitalist economy. However, their assimilation into the "neoclassical synthesis" has obscured, and even suppressed, their revolutionary aspects. Consider Robinson:

After the war, Keynes' theory was accepted as a new orthodoxy without the old one being rethought. In modern textbooks, the pendulum still swings, TENDING towards its equilibrium point. Market forces allocate given factors of production between alternative users, investment is a sacrifice of present consumption, and the rate of interest measures society's discount of the future. All the slogans are repeated unchanged.

Robinson (1973) p. 172

The synthesis or consensus which prevailed at least until the mid-1960s and was used to exposit Keynesian ideas in fact contained little of the Keynesian view of the world. The synthesis which is discussed, usually in the form of the IS/LM framework, in any number of textbooks (Morgan (1978), Harris (1981), Sawyer (1982), Pierce and Shaw (1974) etc.) does include some of Keynes' innovations. The multiplier and the concept of effective demand have underpinned both the theoretical and policy exposition of macroeconomics. This has generated an enormous literature on consumption, investment and even money demand functions at the aggregate level. However, many essential features have been compromised or even excluded.

First, Walras' Law is used as the basic principle linking together the goods market, the labour market, the bonds market and the money market. Essentially this requires that the sum of excess demands and supplies over all markets must be identically equal to zero. Thus for unemployment to exist (i.e. an excess supply of labour) then, by Walras' Law, there must be an excess of demand over supply in one, or more, other markets. Thus, Walras' Law is used to replace Say's Law so that all markets can be included in the aggregation. Keynes' criticism of Say's Law is valid only in that it examines aggregation over commodities alone. So, if there is an excess demand for money, there will necessarily be an excess supply of goods, investment and/or employment. Thus an unemployment equilibrium can be created temporarily through ineffective demand. However, the concept of involuntary unemployment sits very uneasily within the synthesis; indeed the concepts of planned supply and demand are perhaps inappropriate in a monetary economy.

Second, the concept of effective demand and the multiplier are seen as important for the macroeconomy, and macropolicy in particular, but the level of autonomous expenditure and its multiplier effects cannot be viewed as exogenous. Instead, they are to be located within a general equilibrium conception of all macroeconomic aggregates. Thus, the problems of crowding out, dampened multipliers and of the viability of quantity constraints within a Walrasian general equilibrium system are raised. We return to these in the following chapter where the progress of monetarism is charted.

Third, and perhaps most damaging to the presumed generality of Keynes' concept of involuntary unemployment, is that the synthesis made the Keynesian regime a special case of the classical system. Any divergence from full employment equilibrium must be temporary unless there exist market rigidities restricting the movement of the appropriate prices. This focused attention either on: price or wage rigidity so that the price level does not fall; or on the interest inelasticity of investment, such that when the rate of interest falls in response to a declining demand for money and level of inactivity, investment does not increase. Within the synthesis prices are still presumed to react faster than quantities (to disequilibria). Thus, if there is excess supply in the goods market, the absolute price level will fall and equilibrium will be reestablished. This is achieved via the Pigou Effect in the goods market (deflation increases the real value of money and assets and so leads to a positive wealth effect on consumption), and the rise in the real value of the money supply in the money market which pushes down the interest rate. This too raises aggregate demand. The rigidity argument was also applied to both prices and interest rates: wage and price rigidity could occur in the case of absolute liquidity preference (the liquidity trap). Thus, the very construction of the synthesis around Walras' Law and the Pigou Effect reinstated the proposition that if the price level were flexible, involuntary unemployment could not occur in an equilibrium. Keynes' theory was no longer general since it depended on the assumptions of price or interest rigidity, which were empirical causes of disequilibrium readily recognised by classical economics. Thus, while the synthesis incorporated ideas such as the rejection of Say's Law, the importance of money and effective demand, it retained the idea of "quantity responding to price" and the classical workings of the market mechanism.

What is important about the synthesis is that it is a simplified general equilibrium system in which money exists as one of the markets, although money is best conceived of as something which gives transactional services and around which speculative activity is focused. Despite enormous theoretical and empirical effort in the postwar period to construct macroeconomic aggregates such as the consumption, investment and demand for money functions, this general equilibrium character of the synthesis implies that it is conceptually dependent on aggregation from microeconomic foundations and dependent on an individualistic basis. This property is more explicitly shared by the reinterpretation, or reappraisal, of Keynes associated intially with Clower (1965) and Leijonhufvud (1968).

THE REAPPRAISAL OF KEYNES

Perhaps the most distinguishing feature of the Keynesian model, which evolved from the 1930s through to the 1960s, is its attempt to contain Keynes' theories within the Walrasian general equilibrium framework. The conventional Walrasian model embraces an almost instantaneous adjustment of prices to their equilibrium levels, and the adjustment of quantities to prices. Since the mid- to late-1960s, however, there has been a Keynesian reaction to this attempt to embody Keynesian ideas within what some would argue to be a non-Keynesian model. This reappraisal has attempted to restore some of Keynes' theoretical innovations, and particularly a notion of disequilibrium, while remaining within the framework of general equilibrium theory.

A starting point for the reappraisal has been a reinstatement of the idea that "quantity adjusts to quantity" within the economy, and so sales constraints on the optimising behaviour of agents are admitted. For Leijonhufvud, the issue of price versus quantity adjustment is crucial:

In the Keynesian macrosystem the Marshallian ranking of price-and quantity-adjustment speeds is reversed: in the shortest period, flow quantities are freely variable, but one or more prices are given, and the admissible range of variation for the rest of the prices is thereby limited. The 'revolutionary' element in the General Theory can perhaps not be stated in simpler terms.

Leijonhufvud (1968) p. 52

Also for the more recent theoretical works by Malinvaud the short-run rigidity of prices is central to the modelling of economic behaviour under rationing, or quantity constraints: "short-term quantitative adjustments are much more apparent and influential than short-term price adjustments" and "in the short run, the consistency between individual actions is achieved by adjustments of quantities traded rather than of prices" (Malinvaud, 1977, pp. 10 and 12).

The reappraisal, however, has not been solely concerned with the relative short-term rigidities of price and quantity adjustment. Within the neoclassical synthesis, the question of price rigidity is of great empirical concern since within that framework perfect price flexibility is sufficient for a full employment equilibrium to be attained throughout the economy. What the reappraisal has also attempted to show is that even without price rigidities, there is no tendency towards a full employment equilibrium. This can be understood in terms of Clower's (1965) contribution concerning the dual-decision hypothesis. An agent in the economy, facing a given set of prices, can calculate optimal sales and purchases, and these plans are the notional supplies and demands. However, if these notional demands and supplies are to be fulfilled, they will need to be carried out in an appropriate order, or sequence. If, however, there is a delay in one transaction which prevents the attainment of a subsequent planned transaction, then the agent will be forced to undertake a second optimisation contingent on the exchanges that it has actually proved feasible to make. Clower is thus able to distinguish between notional and effective demands in terms of planned demand versus that demand which is actually possible. Clower conducted his analysis in terms of the consumption function. An individual can first make optimising decisions on the assumption that the only constraint is the real wage; this provides a notional supply of labour and a notional demand for goods. Then, however, the individual finds that actual labour supply is less than notional, and hence must recalculate the demand for goods. Effective consumption is decided upon in the face of effective labour supply. For Clower, the notional demands and supplies are only pertinent if full employment general equilibrium is actually attained. Walras' Law will then hold. However, once involuntary unemployment arises, the economy is in a state of disequilibrium, and Walras' Law does not hold. (See Harris (1981) p. 284 for discussion of this point). Given the dual-decision status of demands and supplies, an aggregation over all agents, in which notional supplies and demands are not realised simultaneously, can produce an unemployment equilibrium in which agents confirm each others' constrained decisions. Note, however, that the theory regarding the maintenance and establishment of unemployment equilibria is unresolved—see Malinvaud (1977) and Hahn (1980) for example.

The above discussion of the incorporation of quantity constraints in the reappraisal has not involved any role for money in the economy. It is consistent with constrained optimisation in a barter economy. Once money is admitted, however, the reappraisal can perhaps best be viewed as a generalisation of the synthesis or a generalisation which allows for optimisation over prices but subject to quantity constraints. The synthesis is a restricted version of the reappraisal; restricted so that notional supplies and demands are effective, and so that quantity constraints are absent because of the pervasiveness of perfect price adjustment (see Fine: 1979).

This acquired generality of the reappraisal, however, is still founded on an aggregation over the price- and quantity-constrained optimising behaviour of individuals. This device is used to create a more adequate basis for the concept of ineffective demand. In this respect, the reappraisal can claim to have incorporated in its interpretation of Keynes an important element of his thought. However, by examining Keynesian problems using such a method, first, important aspects of Keynes' contribution are omitted so that, secondly, the reappraisal, like the synthesis, is unable to break fundamentally from the "classical" economics that was Keynes' target.

For Harris (1983) this reflects Keynes' own method of analysis. Keynes was primarily concerned with market phenomena and these "in principle, revealed all that could be known about the economy". The concern of Keynes, just as of the neoclassicals, was with the interaction of demand and supply, to the neglect of production and other non-market aspects of the economy. The method in Keynes' theory was neoclassical. As such, it could readily be absorbed, with the suppression of its innovatory elements, into the mainstream synthesis. With the reappraisal, the emphasis may have changed slightly in that the new "reappraisal synthesis" can now incorporate the neoclassical viewpoint. In either instance, the Keynesian analysis does not present itself as a distinct, innovatory school of thought. The two schools now appear as much of a muchness, to be distinguished only by their belief, or disbelief, in the significance, or existence, of involuntary unemployment and quantity rationing. While these elements may have important and strongly divergent ramifications in both theory and policy, they are both grounded in the aggregation over individualistic optimising behaviour.

The significance of this methodological agreement amongst apparently opposing economic theorists can be readily appreciated by considering the analysis of the many branches of Keynesianism by Coddington (1976) and (1983). The method of analysis of the body of theory which Keynes felt himself to be attacking, can be seen as the analysis of markets on the basis of choices made by individual agents. The resulting theory therefore operates at two levels: individual choice and market phenomena. The two are then related by the analysis of the choices of a representative agent. Such a method of analysis is termed "reductionism" by Coddington since its guiding principle is the reduction of market phenomena to stylised individual choices. Reductionist theory has typically been concerned with equilibrium; this, however, is not a necessary characteristic of reductionism, merely a way of making it more manageable.

Coddington distinguishes three broad varieties of Keynesians; first, fundamentalists (or Post-Keynesians) for whom Keynes' work was a frontal assault on all reductionist theory, and for whom equilibrium theory is an utter distortion rather than a convenient simplification. Secondly, hydraulic Keynesians, who essentially are those who since the war have propagated and popularised an interventionist doctrine, whereby the decentralised economy can be controlled by the government through the manipulation of its own budget. This fiscalist approach is grounded in the central belief that the stable macroeconomic relationships inferred from Keynesian accounting concepts do exist at the aggregate level. Prices and quantities are not separately identified by this approach, since the concern is only with aggregates such as income, output and expenditure. While technically this approach conflicts with reductionism, the difference is really one of emphasis:

> The hydraulic approach shows how things would work when market prices (and wages) will not, or will not quickly enough, or will not be allowed to, perform their allocative role; it analyses a situation in which prices are failing, both as disseminators of information about relative scarcities and in the provision of incentives to act on the basis of that information.
>
> Coddington (1976) p. 1266

The third variety analysed by Coddington is termed "reconstituted reductionism" which refers essentially to the reappraisal school. The writings of Clower and Leijonhufvud are interpreted as an attempt to reassert the discontinuity between Keynesian economics and its alternatives. However, the reappraisal focuses only on the role and usefulness of equilibrium theory. It emphasises the abandonment of the equilibrium concept in favour of the examination of trading at disequilibrium prices and subject to quantity constraints. By so doing, it is claimed that Keynesian ideas are perfectly embraced by such a general (dis)equilibrium framework; all that is required for a rejuvenation of Keynesian theory is a sophisticated rendering of the constraints upon individual choices. However, for Coddington, it is not the equilibrium theorising that is uncongenial to Keynesian ideas but rather the equilibrium trading within the reductionist programme:

> within reductionism everything boils down to acts of choice within a well-specified system of objectives, constraints and forms of interdependence; and in equilibrium theorising we confine our attention to situations in

which all the independently arrived at choices can be simultaneously realised. It then follows that such a system leaves no room for the "unintended" and "involuntary"...

Coddington (1976) p. 1269

Thus it is argued that the accommodation of Keynesian ideas requires either the abandonment of equilibrium or the abandonment of reductionism. The reappraisal examines only the former possibility. We would further argue that the reappraisal is incapable of embracing the truly revolutionary elements of Keynes' *General Theory*. It admits more of Keynes than does the synthesis, but by its adoption of the reductionist method, it is incapable of devising a genuine macroeconomics.

A PERSPECTIVE ON KEYNESIANISM

Both the synthesis and the reappraisal are based upon aggregation from microfoundations. Keynes, however, was concerned to examine the working of the economic system as a whole in a way which divorced the analysis from the necessity for microeconomic foundations. For example, in the case of the financial system Keynes argued by analogy with a beauty judgement contest in which the contestants were required to order the beauties according to what would be the average preference of the contestants. As in the stock exchange, say, it was a question of guessing other investors' intentions. This contained the potential for a whole range of equilibria, particularly at low levels of investment during waves of pessimism, because of the separation of financial decision-making from the realities of investment opportunities. It is this aspect of the economic system which Keynes wishes to bring to the fore, as the context within which individual decision-making is constrained. These properties of the system have to be explored theoretically and empirically rather than be constructed out of the individualistic decision-making of economic agents.

The interpretation of Keynes offered here suggests that the

self-styled school of Post-Keynesians is closest in representing the revolutionary aspect of Keynes' contribution (see
Eichner (1979) and Weintraub (1979)). Both the synthesis
and the reappraisal construct a macroeconomics on
microeconomic foundations, whereas the Post-Keynesians
focus on macroeconomic relations. They emphasise the
existence of money as a social institution and go much
further than Keynes by exploring other economic relations
such as distribution and competitive structure. Here there
is an emphasis upon aggregate economic relations that are
independent of individualistic decision-making: of class
struggle over distribution, of monopolistic mark-up pricing
etc. Economic concepts are used that are constructed on the
grand scale and comparable to those introduced by Keynes,
such as aggregate effective demand, liquidity preference and
the casino-like character of the financial system. The Post-
Keynesians equally have a wish to incorporate recognisable
empirical and historical factors, such as monopoly pricing,
into their concepts, thereby seeking to escape from the
timeless concepts of the orthodoxy.

This praise of the Post-Keynesians is balanced by a critique
in the following part of this book. The point, however, is to
observe that the attempt to identify the "true" Keynes either
absolutely or in terms of a following school is a futile
exercise. Keynes was a product of his time and occupied
something of a half-way house in economic theory, combining a number of different strands that were not entirely
consistent with each other. In order to be persuasive with his
contemporaries he preserved or left unchallenged vast
amounts of the prevailing classical orthodoxy, not necessarily because it was agreeable to him, but more because it
was irrelevant to his purpose to criticise it. This, together
with his emphasis on the significance of money, was all that
was necessary to give birth to the neoclassical synthesis. A
further extension to the reappraisal was required to account
for quantity rather than price-constrained equilibria. Post-
Keynesian economics breaks with both of these schools by
focusing on economic relations in aggregate, but in doing so
exceeds those areas Keynes would appear to have considered

necessary for macroeconomics, because of his primary concern with demand management as the central aggregate relation.

This concern with demand management has dominated conventional analysis of macropolicy objectives, instruments and constraints. It has also governed the conventional analysis of the causes of the long postwar capitalist boom. The dominance of such a fiscalist, or hydraulicist, position within the academic and public arena has bred a neglect of economic theory be it of the sort discussed by Coddington or of the sort we would wish to highlight, termed micro-economics by the orthodoxy. Significantly, this field, which is conceptually one of the two core topics of economic theory, as counterposed to macroeconomics, has enjoyed little or no development in the postwar period. It commands a universal acceptance across competing schools of macroeconomics and, with its stagnant content, across time as well. Little other than technical, that is mathematical sophistication, has been added to the subject since Marshall's Principles of almost a century ago. This reflects in the modern period the intellectual and ideological dominance of macroeconomics which allows microeconomics to look after itself or rather to follow in its dominant partner's wind. The one exception to this is the recent integration of micro and macro claimed by the disequilibrium school which follows the reappraisal tradition. As Coddington's cleverly chosen terminology suggests, this claim leaves something of a distasteful odour, since macro becomes reduced to a quantity-constrained micro.

While the rudiments of conventional demand management may arguably have been assisted by the developments of the reappraisal, the drastic economic changes of the 1970s, noticeably the shift into stagflation, have left conventional Keynesian policy-makers floundering for a convincing explanation of the present crisis. The retort is usually that the economy is not self-righting and that demand management may not be what it once was but is not totally ineffective. In the following chapter we shall return to these debates in the context of the revival of monetarism, but here it should be noted that it appears that Keynesian demand management can in no way justify its often presumed position as the central generator of capitalist economic growth. It is at present on the retreat from its own theoretical weaknesses, which have been exploited by an arguably even thinner theoretical tradition—monetarism—and from its own evident inability to cope with an economic depression, a failure that is surely inconsistent with its position in the intellectual vanguard of capitalist economic prosperity.

Keynes' policy and political perspectives can be explained in terms of the failure of the economy to generate adequate effective demand, which dictates that the state should intervene to remedy this. Significantly, for Keynes, this would preserve a role for the animal spirits of entrepreneurs without damage to the overall level of economic activity. Interpreted another way, this suggests the efficacy of macroeconomic policy in generating full employment and in minimising the necessity for state industrial policy. Consequently, for Keynes as for Keynesianism, attention is diverted from analysis of industrial structure and policy as important determinants of economic performance. This is reflected in the low status and development of microeconomics and its inadequacy in dealing with stagnation.

At the very least, this implies that economics will fail to comprehend the causes of the stagnation of the 1970s just as it has failed to comprehend the causes of the boom that preceded this. The boom allowed us to believe that Keynesianism was its source and that microeconomics was appropriate to its purpose in the healthy aggregate environment. Just as Keynesianism tended to claim the credit for the post-war boom, so now it is discredited by stagflation. Far from diverting attention from macroeconomic management, the demise of Keynesianism has witnessed a further denigration of state economic intervention by the rise of monetarism. It would, however, be wrong to place much emphasis upon policy implementation through the influence of macroeconomics. Industrial intervention has been extensive and has a dynamic independent of macroeconomic policy to a considerable degree. Nevertheless, within the realm of economics, and to that extent in the economy itself, Keynesianism has served both to neglect and to hold back industrial policy. The point is not to downgrade macroeconomics and raise microeconomics to a place of prominence, although this would be an advance in the right direction. It is to a reconstruction of economics that we must look, one that is in touch with the economic realities of contemporary capitalism. This is not a blanket appeal for empiricism, although this might also be a step in the right direction, since economists tend to know more about economics than they do about economies. Rather, if we are right in arguing that macro and micro are out of touch with the economy, it is time to construct a conceptual apparatus that is more appropriate. The simplicity, even obviousness, of such a plea is rendered more urgent when we turn to consider the alternative offered by the restoration of monetarism to the centre of academic and political debate.

3 Monetarism

I INTRODUCTION

"Monetarism" as a term describing a body of economic thought was first coined at the end of the 1960s[1] although its modern theoretical origins can be traced back to the quantity theory of money of Fisher, and later of Friedman. It is only in the recent period that it has gained a wider acceptance amongst both intellectuals and policy-makers. Its crowding out of Keynesian ideology has been based upon persistent and, at times, accelerating inflation accompanied by high levels of unemployment. The decline of Keynesianism has been a natural response to conditions of stagflation as macroeconomic policy has been seen to fail.[2] In the previous chapter it was revealed that the great innovations presumed to be embodied in the Keynesian revolution have been cruelly exposed by the closer examination brought about by faltering economic growth. Keynesianism, as a distinct body of thought, has merely rested on the presumption of price and/or wage rigidities as generalised to a monetary economy. Such tenuous theoretical foundations had been bolstered by the policy doctrine of an activist and beneficent government, smoothing the functioning of an otherwise laissez-faire economy through the management of aggregate demand. This complacent edifice has been rudely shattered by conditions of stagflation and the new doctrine of monetarism has gorged itself on the decaying body of the Keynesian conventional wisdom.

The rise to favour of monetarism is undoubtedly best explained by inflationary conditions. Ideologically, monetarism is associated with the quantity theory because each associates an increase in the money supply with an equivalent increase in prices. The quantity theory is the simplest and most appealing explanation of inflation, so that monetarism's association with it is a source of great propaganda value. The irony is, however, that monetarism has long since abandoned the quantity theory so that, like much propaganda, its popularity is in this instance based on deception. But the propositions of monetarism go far beyond the explanation of inflation. Most obviously—and it is in this rather than in their explanation of inflation that it counterposes itself to Keynesianism—monetarism emphasises the benefits of the free play of market forces and the minimisation of state economic intervention. Essentially this proposition is quite independent of the theory of inflation, but the policy prescription of restricting the money supply to control inflation is identified with a withdrawal of state activity. Consequently, laissez-faire policy gains undeserved support from the supposed theory of inflation which links increases in the money supply to increases in prices. In other words, monetarism is ideologically based on a double deception: that the school of thought embodies the quantity theory and that the quantity theory, or at least its proposition concerning inflation, is a rationale for a non-activist state. Whilst these deceptions evaporate in the academic literature—monetarists no longer use the quantity theory and are quite open in their assertion of the benefits of the unregulated market—they have been widely used more generally to justify deflationary policies resulting in losses in employment and living standards.

If, however, the intellectual, rather than the ideological, basis of monetarism does not rest upon the quantity theory, it remains to be explained. The previous paragraphs suggest that the rise of monetarism is due to its ideological advantage consequent on the stagflation in the world economy and the associated discrediting of Keynesianism. Rather than looking at monetarism as an intellectual advance in response to changing economic circumstances, it is better seen as an attempt to restore intellectual respectability to laissez-faire policy in the wake of Keynesian revolution. Ideologically, the quantity theory suffices for this purpose. Intellectually, it does not, since economic theory no longer allows the quantity theory, as we shall explain below.

It is worth summarising our argument. In the simplest Keynesian model, unemployment and inflation are mutually exclusive, since one takes up where the other leaves off around the level of full employment, subject to any "bottlenecks". Within later Keynesian models, increases in demand, however, could be divided into a stimulus to output and stimulus to the price level (the so-called "missing equation" debate),[3] with (inflationary) expectations permitting both unemployment and inflation where previously this had been impossible. Monetarism did not essentially dispute the theory at this stage. In particular, in the theory of Friedman, it accepted Keynesian theory of the demand for money which had the implication of rejecting the quantity theory. What distinguished Keynesianism from monetarism was the relative emphasis on the output as opposed to the price inducing effect of reflationary policy.

Significantly, the introduction of expectations to the theory was the common response to stagflation, and it was one needed more so by the Keynesians than by the monetarists since the latter were inclined to believe that the economy was close to full employment so that inflation could be explained by excess demand. Initially, the debate focused around the trade-off between unemployment and inflation, as controversy surrounded the merits of the Phillip's Curve. Friedman denied such a trade-off, except in the very short-run, once inflationary expectations were accounted for. Even this has proved inadequate to the new school of monetarism (known as the New Classical Economists) who have revised the theory of expectations to deny the effectiveness of microeconomic management in short- or long-run.

In short, whilst the world economy has witnessed dramatic changes in recent years, macroeconomics has essentially responded by introducing expectations as a major component and point of departure from pre-existing orthodoxies. It is scarcely credible that economists should have confronted such major economic events with such a faint response. Even more astonishing is that economics has been reinvigorated by the theory of rational expectations since it releases new ground upon which Keynesian interventionist propositions can be debated. Consequently, monetarism has had three functions. First it has bolstered an ideology that justifies laissez-faire policies, which are interpreted as deflationary macroeconomic management and cuts in state expenditure. In practice, monetarist regimes—such as those of Thatcher and Reagan—have been highly interventionist in the economy, particularly when this is not restricted to consideration of macropolicy alone. Second, monetarism has challenged the Keynesian myths outlined in the previous chapter. In so doing, it commands some agreement with our own position. But it is more an identity of opposites, since the monetarist position abandons the need for an analysis to replace the vacuum created by the shattering of the Keynesian mythology. Those who believe in the efficacy of laissez-faire effectively undermine the need for economics other than to root out market distortions. Third, monetarism has lent economics, as an academic discipline, a new lease of life. Keynesians and monetarists can debate old controversies anew, doing so today on monetarist terms which now encompass rational expectations.

II A VARIETY OF MONETARISMS

The past ten years have witnessed a revival of monetarism but, because this school of thought has a history and changes over time, it is not a uniform doctrine. However, in the variety of monetarisms, a number of common elements can be discerned. Perhaps the key element within the monetarist doctrine is the presumed line of causality running from money stock to the level of nominal income. At the macroeconomic level, change in the money stock is the dominant factor producing fluctuations in nominal national income,[4] (Friedman and Schwartz: 1963). Secondly, there is a presumption that the private sector is inherently stable at full employment. For Friedman and Meiselman (1963) this was represented by a stable demand for money function, which was less volatile than both the Keynesian investment multiplier and consumption function. More generally, the implication is that disturbances in private sector activity are primarily the result of "erratic" changes in the pattern of growth of the money supply. Thirdly, all monetarists would envisage no long-run relation between inflation and unemployment (in Keynesian terms, the long-run Phillips Curve is vertical). Thus, in the long-run, a steady rate of inflation cannot be used as a policy variable to reduce the level of unemployment. This follows from the concept of the "natural rate of unemployment" to which we shall return below.

A fourth common ingredient to monetarisms is the limited role assigned to short-run macro stabilisation policy. For Friedman, it is possible for a Phillips Curve relation to be used in the short-run, albeit at the expense of ever-increasing inflation. Furthermore, Friedman denied the effectiveness of fiscal policy in favour of the efficacy of monetary policy; in terms of the emergence from the Great Depression of the 1930s it is argued by Friedman and Schwartz that

> monetary policy got the economy into the Depression, and not until fiscal policy had had an explanatory effect on money supply could one claim that economic recovery had taken place.
>
> Desai (1981) p. 3

Thus, not only was fiscal policy a limited lever on the economy, but even that ability to influence activity was conditioned by its effect on monetary variables. While Friedman admitted a weak role for state intervention, the new rational expectations monetarists argue that unemployment cannot depart from its natural rate in any persistent fashion, since there is no trade-off at all between the level of unemployment and accelerating inflation. In their conception of the Phillips Curve, for example, this school differs from Friedman in the characterisation of the expectations formation processes. For Friedman, expectations were adaptive, which implies that agents at best modify their expectations relatively slowly in response to changes in the economic environment. Indeed, they may persistently adhere to a belief that could consistently be shown to be wrong. In the Phillips Curve, this would mean that, with ever accelerating inflation, agents would consistently under-expect the actual price level. Under the rational expectations hypothesis:

individuals will not make continuous and systematic errors in forming their
expectations of inflation, as the adaptive expectations hypothesis implies.
Thus there can only be transitory and random deviations between the
actual and expected rates of inflation.

Burton (1978) p. 20

Hence, there can be no short-run use of the Phillips Curve
relationship for there can be no unnoticed reduction in the
real wage, and any active, expansionary state intervention
will result only in more inflation and not a change in output.
The rational expectations monetarists further conclude that
the state can only influence real economic activity if it acts
randomly, since if private agents know the state's intentions
they will offset these through their own accordingly defined
"rational" behaviour. We shall return to debate the rational
expectations literature and its implications for activism
below; our purpose here is to contrast the new doctrine with
that of Friedman. In particular, the contrast highlights the
enhancement of the ideological aspect of monetarism in the
anti-state interventionism of the 1970s.

Further brands of monetarism can be identified. Mundell
and Johnson have been particularly associated with "global"
or "international" monetarism. This approach focused
particularly on the determination of inflation at a world
level. With a world economic order increasingly characterised by an international integration of both product and
capital markets, and in the 1960s accompanied by a fixed
exchange-rate regime, it was considered crucial to view
inflation as a global phenomenon. And for small open
economies, such as the UK, or more frequently in empirical
analyses for the Scandinavian economies, the domestic inflation rate is dictated by the world level of inflation. Without
doubt, this school contributed ideological support to the
adoption of a flexible exchange-rate regime in the 1970s,
since their analysis suggested that flexible rates would make
domestic inflation a matter for national choice, effectively in
the choice of the rate of monetary growth. It also continues
to exert a considerable influence on policy-makers and
analysts since it now serves to emphasise the international
dimension necessary for inflation control. Depending upon

the extent to which the exchange rate is seen to be flexible, it can be argued that any pursuit of domestic expansion by the state will tend to fuel inflation both directly, by the operation of the money stock on prices, and indirectly, by the feedback from a depreciating domestic currency on import prices. The exchange rate in this model adjusts to ensure real purchasing power parity. If the domestic country chooses a rate of monetary expansion in excess of the global average, its exchange rate will depreciate in line with the implied relative increase in domestic prices. This ensures that, in equilibrium, domestic and world prices are equalised in common currency units. This emphasises another aspect of the anti-intervention ideology of monetarism, since one of the standard Keynesian policy instruments, exchange rate devaluation/depreciation, is shown to lead to nothing but higher inflation—it can have no real effects.

As a whole, however, global monetarism has been displaced by the stronger implications of the new monetarists. Other schools can be identified, like the "fiscal" monetarists Brunner and Meltzer, who emphasise particular budgetary controls and the consequences of different forms of government financing, or the "sticky wages" monetarists like Fischer, who emphasise the unemployment costs of monetary deflation, (Burton: 1978). For our purposes, however, sufficient of the common and disparate elements of monetarism have been sketched.

III FRIEDMAN'S CONTRIBUTION

In his attempt to revive the quantity theory, in the wake of the Keynesian revolution, Friedman developed the quantity theory as a theory of the demand for money very much as an alternative to Keynesian liquidity preference theory. In his Restatement of the mid-1950s, Friedman (1956) insists that the quantity theory is primarily a theory of the demand for money rather than a theory of the determination of income, output or prices (since to look at these you must also consider money supply). The demand for money depends on owned resources and on the returns to holding a variety of assets.

Thus

(1) $$\frac{M^D}{p} = f(r, \dot{p}, y, h, \tau)$$

where p is the absolute level, $\dot{p}$ is the rate of inflation, y is real income, h is the ratio of non-human to human wealth, τ is a taste variable and r reflects a range of yields on a number of assets which constitute money and its close substitutes. Explicitly, the demand for money is the demand for real balances and here it is homogeneous of degree zero in both the price level and in income. This simple extension of the quantity theory into a theory of the demand for money was used by Friedman to attack the Keynesian model since, in his formulation, money demand was now an active constituent in the determination of income.

Two essential components in this attack emerged more precisely in the early 1960s (Friedman and Meiselman: 1963 and Friedman and Schwartz: 1963). First, the demand for money function was asserted to be empirically stable in econometric terms. The demand for money function could be estimated empirically using only a few explanatory variables and it would prove to be a stable relationship. Second, it was asserted that the supply of money was autonomous; it is either exogenously set by government policy or determined by variables outside the money demand function. By this method, Friedman assumed a dominant position in the advancement of monetarist doctrine. The method too was central to Friedman's role. Positivism was invoked with its two main elements: deduction from simple (unrealistic) postulates followed by empirical verification. This methodology has arguably achieved an even more important position within conventional economics than has the monetarist orthodoxy. Again, it is a shared concern of both the monetarist and Keynesian approaches.

With money supply exogenous, then in equilibrium

(2) $$\overline{M}^S = M^D = pf(r, \dot{p}, y, h, \tau)$$

From here, Friedman shows that nominal income (Y) is given by

(3) $$Y = Y(r, \dot{p}, y, h, \tau)\overline{M}^S$$

It is then argued that nominal income is proportional to $\overline{M}^S$ if the bracketed variables are determined elsewhere in the system. Nominal income is determined by nominal money. However, the familiar problem arises, as Friedman was well aware, that equation (3) does not indicate the division of any monetary change between quantity and price movements.

In the early 1960s this lack of output determination remained unresolved. In these, what might be seen as the dark ages of monetarism, the objectives were principally to undermine Keynesian activism. In conjunction with his theory of money demand, Friedman (1957) launches into the Keynesian consumption function with his concept of permanent income. Spending depends on lifetime, or permanent, income and any deviation of spending from its long-run level will be due to the effects of transitory components in income. For Keynes, the marginal propensity to consume was positive but less than one. Keynes also proposed that the marginal propensity to consume was less than the average propensity, on the grounds that the average propensity would decline as income rose. Early long-run time series studies confirmed the Keynesian hypothesis, but this was contradicted by studies of shorter-run movements which showed APC = MPC < 1 (see Wallis: 1979). Friedman argued that if MPC < APC then the income elasticity of consumption must be < 1. Therefore, no stable relation between consumption and income could exist. Such an elasticity of less than one implies that an increase in income would lead to a fall in the APC. Empirically though, the APC appeared broadly constant. It was, therefore, suggested that stability in the APC is in fact inconsistent with stability in the consumption function itself. For Friedman's theory, however, a constant APC was consistent with the permanent income hypothesis but was not required by it. (See Ott, Ott and Yoo (1975) for an interesting discussion of consumption function theories). Friedman's attack on the Keynesian consumption function first argued it to be unstable and so hardly a reliable basis for fiscal activism through the multiplier. Secondly, he was concerned to show an influence for interest rates on consumer decisions.

If interest rates on monetary assets rose then it would be more costly to spend currently on physical consumption.

This effect would also be supported by life-cycle theories of consumption in which national agents will save more when interest rates are high and will spend when it is less costly to do so. Thus if a Keynesian expansion were to generate a rise in interest rates, multiplier effects would be dampened because of the effect on both consumption and investment. However, there is empirical evidence that higher real interest rates also have a wealth or income effect so that consumption actually rises with interest rates.[5]

In short, Friedman was keen to emphasise the stability of the demand for money as a determinant of nominal income and to deny the quantitative significance of the Keynesian output multiplier in the division of increases in nominal income between output and prices. The appeal of the ideas rested upon an uneasy amalgam of theoretical and empirical argument, none of which was entirely satisfactory. The stability of the demand for money function, for example, contrasted with instability in investment and consumption functions. Since the total of these constituted income (and wealth) for each optimising individual, it was necessary for the instabilities in the investment and consumption functions to cancel each other out to give a stable demand for money as residual. Criticisms of this type have persistently been made by Hahn, but they were less necessary whilst Keynesianism enjoyed the centre stage.

Circumstances began to change. Friedman's theory of the determination of output and price by money did not fully emerge and attain wider popularity until the late 1960s, with the development of the expectations augmented Phillips Curve (Friedman: 1968). The Phillips Curve was the principal response of Keynesianism to the inability of its theory to explain the coexistence of unemployment and inflation (and in particular the simultaneous rise in both the inflation and unemployment rates). Statistically, an inverse relationship was observed between the level of unemployment and the rate of wage increases (Phillips: 1958). Theoretically, the relation was explained first in terms of a positive relation between the demand for labour and excess demand for labour, and second that there existed an equilibrium level of unemployment corresponding to frictions in the labour market. Samuelson and Solow (1960) related the level of unemployment (U) and the level of price inflaction ($\dot{p}$) to the rate of wage inflation ($\dot{w}$):

$$(4) \qquad \dot{w}_t = \beta_0 + \beta_1 U_t^{-1} + \beta_2 \dot{p}_t$$

and price inflation to wage inflation and productivity growth ($\dot{z}_t$):

$$(5) \qquad \dot{p}_t = \dot{w}_t - \dot{z}_t$$

From these two equations, a direct relationship between price inflation and unemployment can be derived. In policy terms desired values of U_t and $\dot{p}_t$ can be chosen and then the state can attempt to achieve them through the operation of demand stimuli. A lower level of unemployment can seemingly be achieved at the cost of permanent inflation.

Friedman's attack on this Keynesian formulation was directed towards a technical criticism of (4) and centred on the size of the coefficient β_2. For Friedman, the relevant prices in the wage bargaining process were expected prices, but expected prices that would not be known exactly. Friedman adopted an adaptive expectations process for price expectations $\dot{p}^e$, so that $\dot{p}^e$ is made up of a weighted average of previous price changes. If $\beta_2 < 1$, then agents suffer from money illusion, or their price expectations have yet to catch up with the current rate of inflation. If expectations actually do catch up with the rate of inflation, then the economy can be said to be in a steady state equilibrium. At this steady state, a natural rate of unemployment is defined. With no money illusion, the Phillips Curve is vertical, so that any unemployment—inflation trade-off—can only be a temporary phenomenon. Such a framework can readily explain the coexistence of accelerating inflation and rising unemployment if the government attempts to expand employment beyond its "natural" level. This too completes Friedman's theory of the monetary determination of income. All monetary expansion will ultimately be reflected in price increases and the long-run effect on output is nil. In the long run, output is determined by the "natural" level of unemployment: that level which would be ground out by the Walrasian system of general equilibrium equations, subject of course to the presence of any market imperfections. Effectively, Friedman was applying strict neoclassical theory to the Phillips Curve so that money illusion is eradicated; the equation, therefore, explains the relative price of labour rather than the absolute price.

Many debates have followed Friedman's attack on Keynesianism, to some of which we have already alluded.[6] For our purposes, it is sufficient to relate a number of the theoretical issues which have arisen. First, Kaldor has questioned the line of causality within the restated quantity theory. Even if the presumed stable relationship between money stock and money national income does exist, it has yet to be shown "that the money stock is the exogenous variable and the level of prices and wages the endogenous variables and not vice versa", (Kaldor and Trevithick (1981) p. 3). Further, it is questionable whether changes in expenditure will lead to changes in prices, (as we shall see when we discuss the "Keynesian Dichotomy" below). It is argued that money supply changes may be the result of changes in money demand, and that government influence operates mainly through the subsequent pegging of interest rates. Credit expands merely in response to demand, and so changes in the money supply are endogenous.

The second main assault has come from Hahn, who regards the monetarists as sloppy theorists: "Friedman neither has nor claims to have a monetary theory", (Hahn (1971) p. 61). In particular, there is no specification of a connection between monetary and real changes in the economy; the natural rate of unemployment, as envisaged by Friedman, has never been shown to exist in general equilibrium theory (never mind in the real world). There is little theory to justify either the causality or the concept of equilibrium in his model. Hahn concludes:

There is nothing in what he says to make anyone change his view that changes in the monetary stock exert an influence only if they change people's wealth or interest rates. As far as the theory goes it is only the Pigou effect which had been ignored in the early literature.

Hahn (1971) pp. 79–80

So we are able to conclude this section much as the last; questioning why the monetarist programme has become so important when based upon such dubious intellectual foundations.

The Hahn critique leads us neatly into the next section, which examines the theoretical invalidity of the original "quantity theory". Friedman's specification of monetarism with its inclusion of wealth and interest effects explicitly rejects the "quantity theory" and in fact differs very little from Keynesianism. The same equations can be used to describe either approach; the debate then centres on the size of the Keynesian and monetary multipliers within the real economy. This real economy is determined outside the original "quantity theory" and it is to this issue that we now turn.

IV THE CLASSICAL DICHOTOMY

The quantity theory of money can be used to generate a theory of the absolute price levels; general equilibrium theory can be invoked to generate a theory of relative price determination for the "real" economy in which money is excluded. Walras' Law, which was discussed in a related context in the last chapter, says that the sum of excess supplies and demands over all markets in the economy, including money, must equal zero. If there were aggregate excess demand in one market, there would be an equivalent excess supply in one (or more) other markets. More specifically, if there were nominal excess demand in the n markets (for goods), there would be a nominal excess supply in the n + 1 market (for money). In this form, Walras' Law can be simply derived from an individual's budget constraint: ignoring time, an individual's initial endowments must equal the sum of goods consumed plus the final stock of money balances.

If the homogeneity postulate is added to Walras' Law within a general equilibrium context, then we are able to determine relative prices. The homogeneity postulate says that the demands, and excess demands, in the n goods markets will not change in response to a change in the absolute price level on its own. Essentially this requires that demand (and excess demand) functions are homogeneous of degree zero in money prices (and the associated absolute price level). If relative prices remain unchanged, the demand for a particular commodity should not change in response to a change in the overall price level of the economy. Demand functions for goods are thus dependent on relative prices.[7]

We now have the basic components of a Walrasian General Equilibrium model—excess demand functions, Walras' Law and the homogeneity postulate. Once an equilibrium is also defined as a situation where in each market excess demand is zero then it can be demonstrated that "the n goods markets by themselves cannot determine the absolute price level, p, or the money prices (p_1, ...p_i, ...p_n), but can determine only the n relative prices (p_i/p, ..., p_n/p)." (Harris (1981) p. 56). That is, within such a model, the absolute price level is not determined. An equilibrium is therefore defined only on the set of relative prices, since the absolute price level can have no real effects in this model. A proportionate change in all prices can in no way alter the equilibrium. Thus the quantity theory can be used to determine the absolute price level while the Walrasian general equilibrium model can determine relative prices. However, the integration of these two approaches has proved exceptionally problematical. Patinkin (1965) has shown that if an attempt is made to link a Walrasian general equilibrium model of the physical side of the economy with the quantity theory acting as a determinant of the money market, the resultant model contains an internal inconsistency. This involves an attempt to dichotomise the economy; that is, the economic system is decomposed into two subsystems, each of which is able to function with some degree of autonomy. Problems arise however if an attempt is made to combine the results of these two subsystems. Let us consider Patinkin's proof that the dichotomy proposed is invalid.

There are n excess demand equations, one for each good, where,

$$(6) \quad X_i^{ED} = X_i\left[\frac{p_1}{p}, ..., \frac{p_n}{p}, \sum \frac{p_i}{p} \overline{X}_i^s\right] - \overline{X}_i^s = 1, \quad (i = 1, ..., n)$$

so that excess demand for X_i depends on relative prices, the budget constraints and the fixed supply of $\overline{X}_i^S$. An equation for the absolute price level is given by,

$$(7) \qquad \sum_{i=1}^{n} \Phi_i \frac{p_i}{p} = 1$$

where Φ_i are weights connecting the relative prices to the index p but are unable to define the absolute level of prices.

The quantity theory governs the money market such that,

$$(8) \qquad M^D = kpy$$

which too can be written as an excess demand function,

$$(9) \qquad M^{ED} = kpy - M^S = 0$$

Walras' Law is then used to link the goods and money markets. This law itself can provide an excess demand function for money where,

$$(10) \qquad M^{ED} = - \sum_{i=1}^{n} p_i \, X_i^{ED}$$

excess demand for money is the inverse of the sum of excess demand for goods. Thus, we have two excess demand functions for money, (9) and (10). However, in equation (9) excess demand for money is homogeneous of degree one in absolute prices; that is, if all prices were to double, the demand for money balances would also double. However, in equation (5) the quantity theory indicates that excess demand for money is not homogeneous to any degree. A change in prices will change the demand for money, proportionately, but excess demand will not change proportionately because money supply is unaffected. The two excess demand for money functions are, therefore, mutually inconsistent.[8]

This inconsistency is revealed by the analysis of the two subsystems in a state of disequilibrium. Within the quantity theory, the classical dichotomy is used to show that monetary changes lead to proportionate price changes and the real side of the economy is left unchanged. What Patinkin's result showed was that such a presentation of monetarism, while still common today, is in fact invalid. In the mid-1960s the implication was that all monetarists were, in fact, Keynesians, since monetary changes from whatever source could have real effects. The only real debate concerned the extent to which money stock changes led to output changes rather than price changes. Despite this shattering of the academic respectability of the quantity theory, it has maintained an important ideological and propaganda status. The basic structure of the argument is that money demand adjusts to an exogenous money supply and so leads to the conclusion that monetary expansion causes inflation. This argument has in fact been enhanced by the New Classical school who use this dichotomy in conjunction with rational expectations to show that we are all monetarists!

We shall shortly return to the work of Patinkin in achieving an internally consistent specification of "monetarism" and to Friedman's "new" version of the quantity theory. First, however, we digress briefly to consider the equivalent "Keynesian dichotomy" in an attempt to clarify further the relationship between monetarism and Keynesianism. While in monetarism there is a basic proposition that monetary changes can only lead to price changes, for Keynesianism an opposite proposition is advanced, that any monetary/fiscal stimulus is reflected in quantity changes. This simple point of disagreement effectively underlies the Keynesian position for activism against the monetarist adherence to "sound finance" and anti-interventionism.

It has already been made clear that the case for Keynesian activism is related to its view of the malfunctioning of the capitalist, or market, economy; as in the concept of involuntary unemployment, whether associated merely with price rigidity or with the existence of quantity constraints (if we allow the two to be separate). In terms of the operation of Keynesian demand management, the activist must believe that the central management of public finances will (reliably) affect overall economic activity. In order to justify this position the Keynesians are forced to make their own theoretical dichotomy, to replace the classical dichotomy. This "may be stated as the principle that output is determined by aggregate demand, and that prices are determined by costs" (Coddington (1983) p. 11). This Keynesian dichotomy underpins the case for activism.

This dichotomy provides two subsystems: one where the level of output is determined by demand; and one where the price level is determined by supply phenomena in a manner most explicitly associated with Godley (see Coutts, Godley and Nordhaus (1978) for example). Coddington (1983) denotes these two subsystems as the hydraulic and the markup principles; the former requires that supply is perfectly elastic at the prevailing price and the latter requires that aggregate demand is perfectly inelastic with respect to changes in the price level. Changes in costs, therefore, are only allowed to affect the price level. (The associated Kaleckian dichotomy is effectively very similar to the Keynesian one, but demand is allowed to influence the markup as we shall see below).

Coddington's discussion of the Keynesian dichotomy makes it clear that the hydraulic principle requires that demand for money be perfectly interest-elastic within the IS/LM framework (typically referred to as a horizontal LM curve). Thus the hydraulic principle is operative to the extent that the interest rate is unchanged. Any interest-rate-adjustment is therefore ruled out by hydraulicism. The markup principle on the other hand is based on the observed non-cyclical movement of prices relative to the cyclical movement of unit labour costs. As such it is assumed that prices are set with respect to a "normalised" (or smoothed) labour cost series.

Two main problems emerge from this discussion of the Keynesian subsystems. The empirical validity of the hydraulic principle is dubious. In a large body of empirical research the evidence for the principle rests on higher interest elasticity of money demand at lower interest rates (Morgan (1978), Desai (1981), Pierce and Shaw (1974)), but there is a limit to what can be built upon the (dubious) existence of the liquidity trap. Once monetary expansion is permitted alongside fiscal expansion, interest rates may be stabilised but the physical effects of the expansion may also be eroded. Increases in the price level would need to be continually offset by further monetary expansion (unless of course an incomes, or prices, policy were administered). Secondly, the Keynesian system has no theory of resource allocation, other than the allocation between employment and unemployment. It is this very approach to allocation which ensures that extra resources can always be brought into operation without cost and without generating relative price changes.

This discussion highlights the simplicity behind the Keynesian position of activism. The classical dichotomy first analyses the real and monetary subsystems separately while the Keynesian dichotomy analyses the interaction of monetary and real factors in the first instance and then proceeds to look at phenomena within the subsystems. For Coddington, Keynes' theoretical departure was this replacement or suppression of the classical dichotomy in favour of his focus on the interaction of monetary and real factors. The invalid dichotomy is thus replaced by a new dichotomy which itself is problematical; in particular, the hydraulic principle is the result of the suppression of monetary and budgetary phenomena. Both interest-rate and price-level effects are excluded. Once these are admitted, it becomes apparent that the Keynesian school has little on which to base its definite policy prescriptions, other than the assumptions that prices are not demand-responsive and that interest-rate reactions do not offset the government's fiscal activism. Once again we are left with few theoretical grounds on which to distinguish Keynesianism from monetarism. They are both grounded in their own worlds of expenditure, where they differ only in their emphasis on the effects of that expenditure. The Keynesian dichotomy appears internally consistent, however, unlike the classical dichotomy, but this perhaps is the result of its less ambitious, or non-general equilibrium, specification. In terms of ideology both dichotomies can have a straightforward presentation. That the monetarist ideology should have been in the ascendancy since the late 1960s was perhaps the inevitable consequence of the changed economic circumstances associated with stagflation. For monetarist ideology government spending fuelled by monetary expansion has been the cause of inflation, and once inflation emerged from the economic system Keynesians were left with limited means of dealing with it ideologically when it was accompanied by growing unemployment. For Keynesians, it appeared in a cost-push form, but as is now well recognised, cost-push can only proceed in so far as the state permits it with an accommodating monetary policy. Thus even the Keynesians can end up as quantity theorists! The emergence of accelerating inflation naturally paved the way for the re-emergence of monetarism: indeed, its basic theory is designed to explain little else. That that theory is invalid has not, of course, been at the forefront of economic debate in popular ideology.

Before we proceed to an examination of the more recent developments in monetarist economic thought, we return to reconsider Patinkin's (1965) determination of a general equilibrium monetarist model. The invalid dichotomy shows that the conventional theory of relative price determination cannot be reconciled with the quantity theory's determination of the price level. Having established this, Patinkin proceeded to abandon the homogeneity postulate (and Say's Identity) and so construct a consistent monetary model of relative and absolute prices. Patinkin reintroduces the real balance effect to the excess demand functions. This requires that the demands for both goods and real money balances depend not only on relative prices (and initial endowments), but also on the real value of money balances. *Ceteris paribus*, an increase in the real value of money balances will cause an increase in the demand for goods. By writing the demand for goods to include the real balance effect, it is made to depend on the absolute price level. So if the absolute price level rises, *ceteris paribus*, the value of real balances is reduced, and this reduction will cause a reduction in the demand for goods. The inclusion of this effect of the absolute price level upon the levels of demand ensures that the homogeneity postulate is broken in the goods market. Furthermore, its inclusion implies that a rise in the absolute price level will reduce the demand for all goods, such that all goods are in a state of excess supply.

It can be shown that the Walrasian monetary model with the real balance effect is internally consistent and both money prices and the absolute price level can be determined .[9] This is achieved at the expense of nonhomogeneity in both the goods and money markets. Furthermore, within this model, money is neutral: a doubling of the money supply will lead to a new equilibrium once both money balances and absolute prices have doubled. No real variables are changed. The real balance effect thus emerges as an absolute necessity for the derivation and expansion of monetary theory, since it provides a link between the money market and the goods market.

The real balance effect also came to play a central role within the neoclassical synthesis. Thus, as well as reinstating monetarism with some degree of intellectual respectability, it has also been used to downgrade the strength of Keynesian analysis. There were two main elements within Keynes' argument for an involuntary unemployment equilibrium. First, in the face of an excess supply of labour, the price of labour does not fall. Unemployed workers cannot signal to employers their potential availability for work at a lower real wage, and money wages are relatively sticky in a downward direction because they are, by and large, administered institutionally rather than set by a "free market". Second, even if the price of labour were to fall in response to competitive pressures, employment would still not increase. If money wages were to fall, money prices might also fall, thus leaving output and unemployment unchanged. All real variables in the economy could be left unchanged unless the fall in money wages were to generate a real increase in aggregate demand which would then feed through to the level of employment.

The "Keynes effect" is one way of coping with this situation (see Morgan (1978) p. 88). If wages, prices and income fall in money terms, then the money supply effectively increases in real terms. This may reduce the (transactions) demand for cash and so reduce interest rates (by raising the price of interest-bearing securities). A multiplier effect may then emerge from the effect of lower interest rates on investment and hence an aggregate demand. In this way, wage and price deflation can have effects equivalent to those of an explanatory monetary policy. However, the Keynes effect is neutralised in the presence of the liquidity trap, since interest rates are at their floor.

The real balance effect, however, can be implemented in order to nullify the liquidity trap.[10] By the real balance effect, the real value of wealth is increased by overall deflation. If the absolute price level falls, the real value of all money holdings is increased; it is therefore possible to raise current consumption at the expense of saving. With this line of attack, the monetarists could show that monetary policy's effectiveness exceeded that of simple deflation. This implied that the only cause of unemployment equilibrium within the Keynesian model was the rigidity of wages and prices, since this was the only way to prevent the operation of the real balance effect, and hence the natural tendency of markets to restore themselves to equilibrium. Thus, in terms of theory, despite some Keynesian reservations, the monetarists achieved a supremacy. However, it was also widely accepted that:

> though the real balance effect must be taken account of in our theoretical analysis, it is too weak—and in some cases (due to adverse expectations) too perverse—to fulfil a significant role in our policy considerations.
>
> Patinkin (1976) p. 69

The case for Keynesian activitism is then grounded in the empirical weakness of the forces for wage and price reductions, as well as the maintenance of an environment congenial to entrepreneurial expectations and investment:

> In mild and short-lived recessions, investment is buoyed by belief that high employment and prosperity are the long term norm. Once this confidence is destroyed ... it is terribly difficult to revive it. The practical moral is that active policy, along with market response, is part of the social mechanism for maintenance or restoration of equilibrium.
>
> Tobin (1980) p. 19.

Thus the real balance effect has both buoyed the theoretical development and the ideological advances of monetarism. While it appears very Keynesian, for Patinkin it represented the foundation required for the reconstruction of monetary theory.

Before examining rational expectations monetarism, it is interesting to record Johnson's (1971) views on the reasons for its future decline. The Keynesian orthodoxy had obviously been vulnerable to attack given the failures of economic policy-making, and monetarism had benefited from inflation, which appeared as a more important problem in the public arena than unemployment. Johnson (1971) actually felt that monetarism would itself be displaced because; inflation would be perceived as less of a problem than unemployment; monetary theory was inadequate because it did not explain price versus output adjustment, and it relied on positivism, which enabled it to use simple proxies to complex real world phenomena on an "as if" basis.

In Tobin's (1981) review of the same question, it was suggested that the same problems (the intellectual inadequacies, such as the missing equation, and the absence of structural modelling) remained but that the monetarists had succeeded in dominating the Keynesian orthodoxy and drawing it very much closer to the monetarist methodology. There have been distinct ideological advances for the monetarists over the past ten years, in part to do with disappointing economic performance, particularly continued inflation which has been popularly identified as the principal economic ill. This has, ironically, assisted the monetarist advance since:

There has always been a tension between ideological monetarism, which promises to rescue us from inflation, and theoretical monetarism, which says that inflation has little or no effect on the real performance of the economy.

Tobin (1981) p. 35

This tension, is in fact heightened in the new monetarist tradition which has made a major contribution to the new dominance of monetarism. The strong propositions that have emerged here have left the cosy synthesis way behind, and it is to these that we now turn.

V RATIONAL EXPECTATIONS AND MONETARISM

At the heart of the rational expectations critique of macroeconomics, initiated by Lucas (1972) and (1976), is the claim that macroeconomic policy, whether fiscal or monetary activism, is highly unreliable and unwieldy. Therefore its pursuit will lead not to the predictable consequences envisaged by Keynesian hydraulicists (or even those envisaged by Friedman), but only to an increase in the level of confusion amongst the private sector regarding what is happening in the economy. At best, fiscal and monetary policies can have no effects on real variables in the economy; at worst their effects are totally unpredictable. The most basic insight of this school emerges in the attack on conventional econometric modelling, and particularly on its use for policy-making and simulation. It is argued that the structural behaviour of private-sector agents is not invariant to changes in the public sector's policies. Private-sector behaviour is affected by the present expectations of future economic variables. Thus, if changes in the state's behaviour alter expectations of the future, then if a model neglects this role of expectations, it is likely to give incorrect forecasts. Thus, to model the impact of a change in state economic policy on the economy the reaction of private-sector agents to that change in policy must also be incorporated.

This problem of the internal consistency of econometric modelling has been one line of attack. Lucas and Sargent (1979), in particular, condemn conventional models as being "of no value in guiding policy", and, further, say that their application was extremely misleading in underwriting the role for activism when really such activism was destabilising the economy. The theoretical implications of the rational expectations hypothesis have been well taken by the profession, and expectations are now playing a significant and extensive role in monetarist and non-monetarist model-building alike. That this should be the case is quite illuminating. It suggests either that rational expectations *per se* need to be no more monetarist than Keynesian, or that, once again, the monetarists are dictating the areas of debate between themselves and the Keynesians. If rational expectations alone are not necessarily monetarist, their importance for economic theory becomes striking once they are combined with the instantaneous adjustment to a natural rate of unemployment.

In fact, the starting point for Lucas' critique was the Friedman version of the Phillips Curve. As mentioned above, Friedman relied on an adaptive expectations model for the generation of price expectations. This can be written as:

(11) $$\dot{p}^e_{t+1} = \lambda \sum_{i=0}^{\infty} (1-\lambda)^i \dot{p}_{t-i}, \ 0 < \lambda < 1$$

where $1 - \lambda$ is the rate of decay in the importance of past information to present forecasts.[11] For Lucas this version of expectation formation is simply not rational, and as Friedman himself had pointed out, the Phillips Curve could be exploited in the short run only so long as expectations were proved wrong. Under accelerating inflation, adaptive expectations will always under-forecast actual inflation. With an appeal to rational expectations,[12] the Lucas model is able to argue that any non-rational expectation-generating scheme (such as adaptive expectations) will be consistently in error, and as such would be abandoned by rational economic agents. The second element in Lucas' Phillips Curve is the specification of the instantaneously adjusting, "surprise" labour supply function (Lucas and Rapping: 1969). Let us consider a labour market where the suppliers of labour do not know the price level, while employers do have the relevant information. Let labour supply be

(12) $$L^s = \phi_0 + \phi_1(\omega_t - p^e_t)$$

and demand

(13) $$L^d = \gamma_0 - \gamma_1(\omega_t - p_t)$$

so that supply depends on the expected real wage, but demand depends on the actual real wage. Under market clearing, equilibrium is achieved at full employment where labour supply equals labour demand. That is:

(14) $$\phi_0 + \phi_1(\omega_t - p^e_t) = \gamma_0 + \gamma_1(\omega_t - p_t)$$

From here it can be shown that the real wage is given by:[13]

(15) $$\omega_t - p_t = \frac{\gamma_0 - \phi_0}{\phi_1 - \gamma_1} - \frac{\phi_1}{\phi_1 - \gamma_1}\left(p_t - p^e_t\right)$$

Thus, the real wage deviates from its equilibrium value to the extent that prices deviate from their expected value. If prices as perceived by labour suppliers are less than their true value, then labour supply will rise above its equilibrium value because the real wage is perceived to be higher than it really is. So suppliers are "fooled" into supplying extra labour, and employment increases. With Friedman-type agents such a process could happily persist, but under rational expectations, agents will discover that they have previously made erroneous forecasts and that their real wage is in fact lower than they had anticipated. While there is no theory of learning nor of the acquisition of information,[14] it is apparent that with the rational-expectations assumption, agents cannot persistently be fooled. Indeed, employment can only be raised above its natural rate if agents make mistakes. This approach to the Phillips Curve corresponds to a particular version of equation (4) above. The Lucas and Rapping (1969) analogue is:

$$(16) \qquad \Delta U_t = \beta_1(\dot{\omega}_t - \dot{p}_t) - \beta_3 \dot{p}_t - \lambda U_{t-1}$$

where $1 - \lambda$ is still the speed of adjustment of adaptive expectations.[15] Full rationality requires $\beta_3 = 0$. It should be noted that the Phillips Curve causality is reversed for Lucas since real wage inflation is the cause of unemployment, which in turn corresponds to both movements in short-run labour supply and in output. Once adaptive expectations are fully abandoned (16) is no longer directly relevant, however, and instead by combining (13) and (15) we obtain, in equilibrium:

$$(17) \qquad L^s = L^d = \gamma_0 - \gamma_1 \left[\frac{\phi_0 - \gamma_0}{\phi_1 - \gamma_1} - \frac{\phi_1}{\phi_1 - \gamma_1} \left(p_t - p_t^e \right) \right]$$

Under rational expectations $p_t^e = E(p_t \mid \Omega_{t-1})$, that is the (mathematical) expected value of p_t is conditional on information available at $t - 1$. The gap between p_t and p_t^e cannot, therefore, be systematic since this gap has the statistical properties of a zero mean and a finite variance.

This is the essence of rational expectations.[16] Once agents' rational expectation formation processes are admitted to the Phillips Curve analysis, the exploitable unemployment-inflation trade-off disappears because on average agents will know both the real wage and the natural rate of unemployment. In terms of government policy more generally, the critique is used to downgrade the potential for activism. Government policy is at best neutral in a world of rational expectations and clearing markets. The new view of monetarism thus differs enormously from Friedman's: while for Friedman only money mattered, for new monetarists no macroeconomic policy can systematically have real effects on the economy; Friedman favoured stable monetary growth but the new view suggests that any predictable policy is the same as any other; for Friedman, activist policies might be effective but were not desirable, while for the new view there are no disequilibria in the economy, and no government action can assist the natural speed of adjustment between equilibria.

These projections from the new monetarists depend on the twin pillars of rational expectations and continuous market clearing. There is a general agreement that it is the latter which is most important for the school's radical policy implications (Tobin (1980), Buiter (1980)). In policy terms the rational expectations hypothesis makes the point that the structure of economic behaviour depends on expectations about policy. The multiplier as estimated under one policy regime, for example, may not be relevant to a subsequent period when an alternative policy is in operation. A prime example of such "instability" is in fact the Phillips Curve; conventional estimates of the extent and level of the unemployment-inflation trade-off in the 1960s were no longer relevant in the inflationary 1970s. This might simply be because of the neglect of expectation formation (although it might also be that no such relationship has ever existed!). The continuous market clearing concept, however, underlies the stronger proposition of the new school, that once government policies are fully expected and understood by the private sector, they can have no real effects since agents will offset them in order to remain at the real positions they wish to achieve.

For fiscal policy, the argument has developed into the area of the Ricardian Equivalence Theorem. In this context, the debate centres on the effectiveness of substituting bond finance for taxation in the financing of the government's deficit. Ricardo's argument that taxes are merely deferred by bond financing has been revived (Barro (1974) and Artis (1979)). The re-emergence of this debate again reflects the demise of Keynesian theory; for hydraulic Keynesians expansionary fiscal policy can raise aggregate demand, output and employment and the financial consequences are ignored. Barro has reinstated the "crowding out" debate whereby the choice of financing may inhibit the potential of fiscal policy. If bond financing implies a corresponding increase in future tax payments, then the issue of bonds cannot imply a rise in net wealth. For Keynesians, the retort has centred on "tax illusion" (do agents fully discount taxes?) and second that the view that bonds have to be financed by taxes implies that the economy is at full employment. The latter is the more interesting since it implies that in an unemployment equilibrium, bond-financed expansion can generate real income increases. Thus, the standard Keynesian-monetarist "controversy" regarding involuntary unemployment and price rigidity underlies one of the "new" monetarist propositions.

As regards money financing, the argument is stronger. In response to a monetary expansion, agents can only stay at their preferred "real" positions by scaling up all absolute prices, leaving relative prices unaltered. This can of course be carried out if monetary changes are correctly forecast. Tobin (1980), however, makes two objections: if a monetary increase leads to the expectation of an increased price level, this is a real change to the extent that it will affect the real rate of return on money; second, if there is a one-off rise in money supply, which is used to repurchase government bonds, this too will have real effects through its effect on wealth composition:

The only neutral way to engineer a change in the quantity of money, neutral whether anticipated or not, is trivial; it is to decree a scalar change in the monetary unit of account, making old francs into centimes and one hundred old francs into new francs.

Tobin (1980) p. 32

It is apparent that Keynesians feel able to cope with the simple rational expectations critique, since it can either be incorporated by the addition of expectational processes or by the return to established areas of debate.

The second element—continuous market clearing—is also a return to an old issue. It provides however a much stronger vision of the capitalist economy. It is a return to the idea of Walrasian general equilibrium, but it asserts that the state of market clearing equilibrium is continuous. Disequilibria cannot occur. As a result of this clearing, unemployment in the labour market must be voluntary. Thus, there is no Phillips Curve trade-off even in the short run. In the Lucas model (above) employment can only be raised above its natural level if errors are made on the supply side. Faced with the resurgence of this conception of the economy, Keynesians have adopted a number of responses.

One is to attack the Walrasian foundations of the model, another is to attack the *ad hoc*ery of Lucas' specification and the last is to develop their own rigorous (mathematical) models of Keynesian disequilibria. For Hahn (1980), the Walrasian concept cannot model the important (Keynesian) microeconomic market failures. It is the adoption of the Walrasian system which underlies the monetarist proposition that systematic policies cannot affect the "natural" values of real economic variables. Once an attempt is made to incorporate involuntary unemployment in a Walrasian context, without the assumption of perfect competition, then there is scope for effective government policy.

Hahn (1980) and (1982) has catalogued the theoretical inconsistencies and unreliability of the new monetarism just as he previously denounced Friedmanite monetarism. The natural rate of unemployment remains an "unproven assertion". The rational basis for agents' rational mistakes is as yet *ad hoc*; somehow government policy causes people to make errors. Similarly, there is still no theory to support the view that a monetary injection will lead only to higher prices and wages. Such an outcome is just one possibility. The new monetarism has not answered the old "missing equation" argument, it has merely defined it away. It is here that Hahn has an interesting argument. In the case of fiscal activism, the Keynesian expectation is that government policy will have real effects, but may also lead to a slight rise in prices. If there is wage (union) resistance to price rises then it is not rational to expect the policy to have real effects. However, wage resistance will also damage the monetarist propositions. The real wage cannot be reduced, so monetarist deflation will not act to raise employment. In such a case, there is no equilibrium without involuntary unemployment. So both Keynesian and monetarist policies would be ineffective if these problems underlie the present recession.

The new monetarist theory awaits a rigorous general equilibrium specification just as Keynesian models of unemployment disequilibria are yet to be fully expounded. At a theoretical level we confine ourselves to one comment on the content of the rational expectations critique. In the wake of the closer examination of rational optimising behaviour by individuals, mathematical economics has given birth to a new field of theoretical literature, on the problem of incentive compatibility. Essentially, it deals with the problem of individuals misrepresenting their preferences in the market or elsewhere (such as voting) in order to gain an advantage. Most obviously, in voting for example, if you think your most preferred candidate cannot win, you misrepresent your preference by voting for your second choice. This might be considered unfair and is liable to upset the best intentions in laying down a decision-making mechanism designed to choose an optimum choice relative to genuine preferences.

Now, exactly the same problem can occur in the market place. A supplier, for example, in reporting to the Walrasian auctioneer, might misrepresent preferences or technical possibilities in order to gain a price increase or output reduction. Such are the well-recognised problems of central planning, but they also correspond to oligopoly behaviour. But what has this to do with the new monetarism? Well, it poses considerable problems because the rational expectations hypothesis is associated with the assumption that each agent has an equally satisfactory model of the workings of the economy. With instantaneous market clearing, this leads to full employment etc. subject to systematically predictable government policy. This is true, however, only in so far as agents represent their true preferences in the market place.

Why, as rational well-knowing individuals, should they do this? There is little or no reason at all, for they are liable to be aware of false-preference representation which will be to their immediate advantage. Only under extremely restrictive conditions, with infinitesimally small chance of these conditions holding, would rational individuals actually behave perfectly competitively. The rational expectations hypothesis leads to chaos since the natural rate of unemployment is not incentive-compatible.

We are beginning to feel a little guilty, and the preceding paragraphs reveal a large tongue pushing cheeks to breaking point. By bringing together a variety of contributions to economic theory, we have produced absolute nonsense. This is little more than is to be expected from the ingredients: rational expectations for which economic agents wander around with econometric models of extreme sophistication in their heads, instantaneously clearing markets and incentive incompatibility. This is the world of ideas inhabited by economists. We must apologise if at times we embrace its apparent insanity.

Nevertheless, at the policy level the monetarists have made distinct advances despite the theoretical issues challenged by writers such as Hahn, Tobin and Buiter. At a policy level, conventional proponents of demand management have been left in very uncertain terrain. For writers such as Budd (1978) and Blackaby (1978) it has become increasingly difficult to manage economic policy successfully. For Callaghan in 1976 it must have appeared more than "difficult":

> We used to think that you could spend your way out of a recession, and increase employment by cutting taxes and boosting Government spending. I tell you in all candour that that option no longer exists, and that insofar as it ever did exist, it only worked by injecting a bigger dose of inflation into the economy, followed by a higher level of unemployment as the next step. Higher inflation followed by higher unemployment. We have just escaped from the highest rate of inflation this country has known; we have not yet escaped from the consequences: high unemployment. That is the history of the last twenty years.[17]

At the other extreme, monetarists such as Mascaro and Meltzer (1983) suggest that it is the very unpredictability of

US monetary policy that has caused the recession since 1979; the added uncertainty has raised the demand for money and put a premium on interest rates leading to a fall in economic activity.

The whole of this debate, however, has been undertaken over a very narrow range of phenomena. From the earliest monetarist critique of Keynesianism, the questions asked have concerned only the effects of the various expenditure aggregates. The revitalisation of the debate by the new monetarist school has served precisely to show how little of the economy is embraced by "macroeconomics" and how out of touch with the workings of the economy is the discipline. This is most apparent from the highly rarified assumptions adopted by the new monetarist school: rational expectations and continuous Walrasian equilibrium. The focus upon the reaction of private-sector agents to government policy is no doubt an important contribution, but within the format of the monetarist-Keynesian orthodoxy its importance is overstated by the artificiality and unreality of the whole construct.

While we would reject the monetarist framework of analysis, we do find ourselves in affinity with some of its propositions. We do not believe that Keynesianism caused the postwar boom; we would agree with the monetarists that it had an uncertain effect. It may have laid down some of the conditions necessary for rapid economic expansion, but it was not the principal cause of capitalist development. It may well have been destabilising at other times as well. We would disagree violently with the monetarists, however, in their ascribing the postwar boom to the more or less automatic harmony of the laissez-faire economy. Such an economy can only be anarchistic and dominated by "market failure" and economic crises. We should also disagree with the monetarist prescription for a neglect, and even withdrawal from industrial policy. Their critique highlights the neutrality of the composition of government intervention for both Keynesians and monetarists.

It has been argued here that monetarist and macro-economic theory have diverged drastically from capitalist economic reality. We turn now to consider the Kaleckian tradition in some detail. This tradition has always sought a consistency between its theory and empirical phenomena. However, it will be argued that this school too maintains a focus on essentially Keynesian demand concepts, alongside monopoly, and that as such it cannot give a full understanding of the workings of the capitalist economy.

NOTES

1. See Brunner (1968), Purvis (1980) and Desai (1981).
2. See for example Morgan (1978).
3. See for example Stein (1976).
4. This is what Burton (1978) refers to as "impulse dominance".
5. The interested reader is referred to Davis (1982), Wickens and Molana (1982), Muellbauer (1983) and Hendry (1983) for some recent discussions of the consumption function and, in particular, of interest-rate effects.
6. See Desai (1981) and Harris (1981).
7. See Deaton and Muellbauer (1980) for extensive discussions of homogeneity in a microeconomic context.
8. See Weintraub (1979) and Harris (1981) for some discussion of this invalid dichotomy between the real and monetary sectors.
9. Patinkin (1965) and Harris (1981).
10. See Patinkin (1976) for an extended discussion.
11. See for example Pindyck and Rubinfeld (1976) p. 428, or Fleming (1978) for some discussion.
12. Specifically, those forecasts generated by a rational, expected utility-maximising decision process in which the costs of acquiring and processing information are balanced against the anticipated benefits from further improvements to the forecast. The classic reference in this area is Muth (1961).
13. Dropping unnecessary t subscripts:

$$\phi_1\omega - \gamma_1\omega = \gamma_0 - \phi_0 + \phi_1 p^e - \gamma_1 p$$

$$\omega = \frac{\gamma_0 - \phi_0}{\phi_1 - \gamma_1} + \frac{\phi_1}{\phi_1 - \gamma_1} p^e - \frac{\gamma_1}{\phi_1 - \gamma_1} p$$

$$\omega - p = \frac{\gamma_0 - \phi_0}{\phi_1 - \gamma_1} + \frac{\phi_1}{\phi_1 - \gamma_1} p^e - \frac{\gamma_1}{\phi_1 - \gamma_1} p - p$$

$$= \frac{\gamma_0 - \phi_0}{\phi_1 - \gamma_1} + \frac{\phi_1}{\phi_1 - \gamma_1} \, p^e - \left[\frac{\gamma_1}{\phi_1 - \gamma_1} - \frac{\gamma_1 - \phi_1}{\phi_1 - \gamma_1} \right]$$

$$= \frac{\gamma_0 - \phi_0}{\phi_1 - \gamma_1} - \frac{\phi_1}{\phi_1 - \gamma_1} \left[p - p_e \right]$$

14. See, however, Grossman (1981) who examines the acquisition of information and the question of the existence of equilibria where price conveys information.
15. Desai (1981) p. 79 for an extensive discussion of these relationships.
16. See Oxley (1983) for a survey of the recent rational expectations literature.
17. Quoted, amongst other places, in Blackaby (1979).

PART II

Introduction

The previous part has been devoted to a critical assessment of modern macroeconomics. It has questioned the extent to which it is "in touch with reality" both in terms of its divorce from the nature of the way that modern capitalism has developed and in terms of its capacity to regulate that development. Whilst macroeconomics has dominated orthodox thinking, it has not stood alone on the stage of economic thought. A school of thought that can be traced to the work of Kalecki has maintained a radical tradition. It has the advantage of claiming a theoretical correspondence to empirical developments within modern capitalism. It emphasises that economic relations have increasingly been influenced by monopolisation. The result within each sector of the economy is for output to be restricted and for prices to be higher. Ultimately, this leads to a distributional shift of income against consumers, restricting the demand for final consumption goods. Investment is also moderated by the oligopolistic structure of industry. Restrictions on investment and consumption are in turn a source of deficient demand in the Keynesian sense so that the monopolised economy is perceived to be subject to stagnationary tendencies.

This approach demonstrates some sharp differences with the orthodoxy. It places the monopolisation of the economy in a central position and, in this sense, the economics of industry enters into the analysis of the economy as a whole. It is also concerned with macroeconomic aggregates in class terms. Effective demand is formed out of expenditures from wages and profits, with the former distributionally restricted by the overall degree of capitalist monopoly power. These features of the theory have led it to be identified with Marxism. Many of its proponents such as Kalecki, Steindl (1952) and Baran and Sweezy (1966) are sympathetic to

Marx's thought. Yet their central proposition remains that the analysis contained in Marx's *Capital* is no longer appropriate to an understanding of the modern economy in which the monopoly of the twentieth century has displaced the free competition of the nineteenth.

Such judgements are often hastily made with only an imperfect acquaintance with Marx's economics, for it is clear enough that Marx was aware of and even assigned a central place in his analysis to the process of monopolisation. The same is true for other writers in the Marxist tradition, such as Lenin, for whom imperialism, as the highest stage of capitalism, is mostly succinctly described as the monopoly stage.[1] However, even if account is taken of the presence of monopoly in the classic economic works of Marxism, it is often still argued that its theoretical tools remain deficient. The same position is adopted in relation to macroeconomics and to the neoclassical notion of perfect competition, and its associated general equilibrium, in which full employment and efficient allocation of resources prevail.

In this part, we show that Marxism can accommodate the phenomenon of monopolisation without abandoning the basic theoretical propositions of *Capital*. We present this by way of a conclusion to an analysis which is more concerned with developing a critique of the Kaleckian tradition. The intuitive appeal of this latter approach is shown to be misleading. Its assumptions are shown to exclude vital economic influences which coerce the accumulation of capital and whose absence is intimately related to the hypothesis of economic stagnation and monopoly as the opposite of competition. Marxist theory rests upon the central role assigned to the accumulation of capital. Consequently, it recognises monopolisation as co-terminous with and not exclusive of competition.

In the next chapter a formal analysis is made of the supply side of monopoly capitalism according to the Kaleckian tradition. This chapter may be omitted by those who are prepared to take the technical results that it contains on trust. The material is more informally discussed in the following chapter together with some modifications and extensions. The same procedure is adopted in the two chapters which then discuss the demand side of this model of monopoly capitalism. Subsequently, demand and supply are put together to constitute monopoly capitalism as a whole. This is discussed in Chapter 8 where it is set against a critical alternative.

Throughout, reference is made particularly to the recent book by Cowling (1982). This does not reflect the lack of other writers in this tradition, for there is the school of Post-Keynesians who share similar views, as well as other leading recent contributors, such as Sawyer (1982). Nor does it represent some vindictiveness against Cowling, by singling him out for comment. Rather, it is more by way of a compliment. This is because Cowling has taken the Kaleckian tradition further than others both theoretically and empirically. At the same time, his argument is centred around the simplest model of monopoly capitalism, where the degree of market power on the supply side complements the lack of effective demand on the demand side. Consequently, he can assess other factors than those accommodated by the simple model for their effects on supply and demand. This simplicity of presentation is a virtue for our purposes. It allows the basic concepts of the model of monopoly capitalism to emerge sharply and to be assessed critically. At the same time the framework of monopoly supply and demand, in which more general economic and social factors are situated, can be examined. However, we stress that there are differences within the school that we are considering, encompassing as it does, Post-Keynesians, Kalecki, Baran and Sweezy and others. But we are concerned to highlight the aspects they share in common—and they are considerable—and refer to differences more for the purposes of exposition than to do justice to the nuances that divide them.

NOTES

1. Significantly, Lenin's (1963) concept of monopoly, like Marx's, is not predominantly focused on the concentration of market shares, which is the primary emphasis of the Kaleckian school.

4 Monopoly Supply Side Economics: A Formal Analysis

I. INTRODUCTION

The motivation behind Kalecki's analysis of the degree of monopoly was to suggest that firms could increase their markup of prices over costs the more concentrated their market power. Ultimately, the overall markup was passed on to consumers who would predominantly be wage-earners, with the profit margins on intermediate products being passed on from one capitalist to another until the products made their way to the market as consumption goods. This suggested a theory of the distribution of income, in which profits gained and wages lost with an increasing degree of monopoly.

The analysis of the distribution of income in terms of the degree of monopoly left the degree of monopoly undetermined, although the analysis was suggestive of factors that would influence the degree of monopoly, most notably the degree of market power through concentration of market shares and the elasticity of demand for consumption goods which might be influenced by advertising. Nonetheless, the degree of monopoly stood more as a tautologous derivation of the markup of prices over costs rather than as an explanation of that markup. Eminent writers in this tradition such as Baran and Sweezy (1966) and Steindl (1952) did not directly tackle this problem. However, recent work by Cowling (1981) and (1982)) has attempted to complete this Kaleckian model of distribution by specifying the relationship between elements of industrial market structure and the share of gross capitalist income in value added in the economy. The result obtained has also been applied to the estimation of interindustry structure-performance relationships (Cowling and Waterson: 1976).

Our point of departure is to examine in detail the modelling undertaken by Cowling. His model brings out most clearly the link between oligopolistic behaviour and the degree of monopoly. Our remarks are confined to the internal logic and the implications of the Cowling formulation alone and consequently the same applies to our results, some of which can be considered an original contribution to the theory. In this chapter then, we work solely within Cowling's model of the economy and attempt to extend its implications to its limits. By this means it is possible to ascertain whether the intuitive plausibility of the approach is borne out by a closer examination. We find that the intuition only survives unimpaired under the most stringent conditions.

We examine the model under three headings: monopoly supply side economics, comparative statics, and stability. In section II we examine the aggregation of the degree of monopoly from the firm to the industry and, in section III, from the industry to the economy level. The degree of monopoly is seen to be determined by the degree of collusion, the degree of concentration, and the price elasticity of demand. At the industry level we demonstrate the limited nature of collusion under consideration: it centres on demand considerations alone but we discuss the possible role of differences in firms' costs. At the economy level we show that no general results can be obtained about the role of the average price elasticity in the aggregate degree of monopoly. However, if we confine ourselves to single own price demand curves, the demand elasticity is unity for every industry and we show that the number of industries is irrelevant to the definition of the aggregate degree of monopoly. We also discuss the further restrictive assumptions required if we are to consider monopoly in a general equilibrium context.

Having established in sections II and III that the equilibrium associated with a colluding industry depends on the degree of collusion and the given cost and demand curves, we examine the comparative statics of the system in section IV. We obtain results concerning the impact of changes in costs, the number of firms (n), the degree of collusion (α), and the inverse price elasticity of demand (e) upon industry output, and then consider how changes in n, α and e might affect the dispersion of market shares. In section V we examine the stability of equilibrium in oligopolistic industries. We analyse stability on the basis that the expected retaliatory behaviour is realised and we consider two possible interpretations of the collusion parameter α; (a) formal collusion, where all other firms act in concert in response to one firm's output change; (b) informal collusion where firms adopt the behavioural rule of retaliating at the rate α whenever other firms change their output. We derive the appropriate stability conditions and find that, under informal collusion, the degree of monopoly diminishes rather rapidly as the number of firms increases.

II MONOPOLY SUPPLY SIDE ECONOMICS: THE INDUSTRY

The formal model of the degree of monopoly begins at the level of the firm and then aggregates to the level of the industry and subsequently to the level of the economy as a whole. Let the ith firm in the kth industry have cost function $F_{ik} + C_{ik}(X_{ik})$ where F denotes fixed costs and C variable costs for output X. Price for the industry is given by p_k and it is the uniformity of price for a homogeneous output which effectively defines the industry as a sector distinct from others. The firm maximises profits by taking account of its own given cost function, its own effect on a downward sloping demand curve and the reaction of other firms in the industry to its output decision. Profit π is given by

$$\pi_{ik} = p_k x_{ik} - F_{ik} - C_{ik}(X_{ik})$$

which is maximised when

(1) $$p_k + X_{ik}\frac{dp_k}{dX_{ik}} - C'_{ik} = 0$$

Now dp_k/dX_{ik} depends on two things. For a unit increase in the firm's supply there is a perceived movement down the industry demand curve. In addition, other firms in the industry are anticipated to retaliate by increasing their output. It is assumed that this is in proportion to the percentage increase in output made by the original firm

$$\frac{dX_{jk}}{dX_{ik}} \cdot \frac{X_{ik}}{X_{jk}} = \alpha_{ijk}, \ i \neq j.$$

We will assume that α_{ijk} is independent of i, j and k. This is implicit in making legitimate any aggregation over firms and/or industries.

Accordingly,

$$(2) \qquad \frac{dp_k}{dX_{ik}} = \frac{dp_k}{dX_k} \cdot \frac{dX_k}{dX_{ik}} = \frac{dp_k}{dX_k} \sum_{j \neq 1}^{n} \frac{dX_{jk}}{dX_{ik}}$$

where there are n firms in the industry. We have

$$\sum_{j=1}^{n} \frac{dX_{jk}}{dX_{ik}} = 1 + \sum_{j=i} \frac{dX_{jk}}{dX_{ik}}$$

which is the total change in industry output in response to a unit change in firms i's output.

$$= 1 + \alpha \sum_{j \neq i} \frac{X_{jk}}{X_{ik}}$$

Thus,

$$(3) \qquad \sum_{j=1}^{n} \frac{dX_{jk}}{dX_{ik}} = 1 + \alpha \left[\frac{X_k - X_{ik}}{X_{ik}} \right]$$

Substituting (3) and (2) in (1) yields

$$p_k + \frac{dp_k}{dX_k} \left(X_{ik} + \alpha(X_k - X_{ik}) \right) - C'_{ik} = 0$$

$$p_k + \frac{dp_k}{dX_k} \left(X_{ik}(1 - \alpha) + \alpha X_k \right) - C'_{ik} = 0$$

It follows that

$$(4) \qquad \frac{p_k - C'_{ik}}{p_k} = -\frac{dp_k}{dX_k} \cdot \frac{X_k}{p_k} \left((1 - \alpha)\frac{X_{ik}}{X_k} + \alpha \right)$$

Equation (4) gives a determinate solution where market shares vary inversely with cost differences among firms. There are n equations of the form (4) and the industry

demand function so there are $(n + 1)$ equations and $(n + 1)$
unknowns (the market shares and total output and the
market price) when there are n firms. There is obviously a
problem of simultaneity: do market shares, collusion and
demand elasticity determine price-cost margins, or do
differences in marginal costs determine market shares? We
take up this point below.

On the conventional interpretations, the degree of
monopoly for the individual firm where e is the elasticity of
demand, is given by

$$\frac{1}{\eta_k}\left((1 - \alpha)\frac{X_{ik}}{X_k} + \alpha\right).$$

It is the inverse of the elasticity multiplied by a weighted sum
of market share and unity. It is accordingly larger, the
greater is market share, the degree of collusion α, or the
inelasticity of demand. The significance of this measure is
that it exists at the firm level and is in principle measurable
subject to the assumptions. (Indeed, this has been the focus
of the papers by Iwata (1974), Gollop and Roberts (1979) and
Geroski (1981), although they do not seem to have considered in any great detail the role of inter-firm cost differences). Everything else follows by aggregation.

The degree of monopoly for the industry is measured by
taking a weighted average of the measures for the individual
firms. A firm with a large market share should count more
and at the same time has a greater degree of monopoly itself.
Let μ be the degree of monopoly, then

(5) $$\mu_k = \sum \frac{1}{\eta_k}\left[(1 - \alpha)\frac{X_{ik}}{X_k} + \alpha\right]\frac{X_{ik}}{X_k}$$

(6) $$= \frac{\alpha}{\eta_k} + \frac{(1 - \alpha)H_k}{\eta_k}$$

where H is the Herfindahl index. This is the formula derived
by Cowling (1982). It is identical to the measure for the firm
except H has replaced market share.

The formula for μ is clearly dependent upon the weights
used to aggregate the individual firm price-cost margins. For
example, if we take the simple average across the industry the

result can easily be seen to be

$$e\left(\frac{(1 - \alpha) + n\alpha}{n}\right)$$

which is identical to the weighted measure of the degree of monopoly when the market shares are equal (for which $H = 1/n$). Here $e = 1/\eta$ and we drop the industry subscript k unless it is specifically needed. The choice of the weights X_i/X for the individual degrees of monopoly is motivated by the wish to capture the aggregate disparity between price and marginal cost. These would be equal for perfect competition. Such a measure is reasonable for a single-firm industry since the monopoly loss is entirely due to output restriction and higher prices (even though it has been traditional to measure the loss by half of surplus profits; see Cowling and Mueller (1978), for example). For oligopoly, however, in which the firms have different marginal costs the source of monopoly loss is two-fold. Apart from higher price through output restriction, there is departure from competitive equilibrium through production taking place at marginal costs that are not equalised. If, for example, marginal costs c_i are constant for the ith firm but differ across firms, efficiency would dictate that all production should take place with the firm with least c_i.

In this light, the formula $\mu = e(\alpha + (1 - \alpha)H)$ can be seen to be a product of the aggregation weights utilised. Other weights would yield a different measure as we have seen in the case of the simple average. To give another example, if we weight by X_i^2/X^2 then we find that the degree of monopoly is measured by $e(\alpha H + (1 - \alpha)M)$, the inverse of the elasticity multiplied by a weighted average of the Herfindahl and Murfinedahl indices where the latter, jokingly named, is the probability that if three units are purchased they all come from the same firm.

This discussion serves to illustrate a further point. The formula $\mu = e(\alpha + (1 - \alpha)H)$ tends to suggest that the degree of monopoly is determined by e, α and H. Nothing could be further from the truth. Of these three, only α is an exogenous parameter. Both e and H are calculated on the basis of firm outputs, $X_1, \ldots X_n$ and total output X and these are in turn derived from given cost functions which, along with n and the industry demand curve, are the only exogenous parameters of the system. It is possible to make any of these endogenous but then the optimisation would change and so would the associated mathematical results.

This discussion can be carried further to demonstrate the limited nature of collusion that has been incorporated within the model. It concerns *demand* considerations alone, the extent to which firms push up price in accord with each other through formal or informal agreements. But microeconomic theory teaches that the costs of production for an industry are minimised when marginal costs are equalised across firms, for otherwise production should be shifted from a firm with high to a firm with low marginal cost. The industry has an incentive to collude to minimise costs in this way whatever the methods of redistributing the gains of the resulting increase in profits. In general, the principle of minimising costs of production within the industry conflicts with the principle of collusion to maximise revenue. It is worth examining conditions under which the two principles are compatible. Within the model of degree of monopoly, equalised marginal costs has the implication of a uniform degree of monopoly across the industry since there is a uniform price. Since e and α are taken to be constant, equalised marginal costs occur at equal levels of output. Identical market shares leads to H taking on its minimum value of $1/n$. On the other hand, the degree of monopoly for the industry is at a maximum when a single firm produces all output so that H equals unity. There is a conflict over the two forms of collusion within the industry, with pressure for minimum costs pressing towards output to be distributed across firms and maximum revenue pressing for a single firm. It is quite arbitrary to presume that collusion to maximise revenue predominates over collusion to minimise costs. That it does so within the model reflects a more general neglect of pressure to reduce costs, in this instance at the level of the industry.

We conclude this section with a simple algebraic result. Since H lies in the range between $1/n$ and 1, corresponding respectively to equal market shares and a single firm, it follows that:

$$(7) \qquad e\left(\alpha + \frac{(1 - \alpha)}{n}\right) \le \mu_k \le 1$$

with μ_k taking on its lower bound when there are equal market shares and the upper bound when either α or H equals unity.

Cowling considers α in the range

$$0 \le \alpha \le 1$$

with $\alpha = 0$ giving the Cournot solution and $\alpha = 1$, that of perfect collusion. However it would seem quite plausible that α might be > 1 or < 0. If it were > 1 we might expect this to represent some form of "super-collusion" where retaliation to output decision is extremely strong; $\alpha < 0$ implies an acceptance of dominant leadership such that rivals make some effort to maintain industry price by *restricting* quantity in response to one firm's increase in quantity. When $\alpha = 1$, it is generally presumed that this is equivalent to pure monopoly. It can be seen that for $\alpha = 1$ all marginal costs must be equal across firms. For variable marginal costs, this is possible with all firms surviving, and yields minimum production costs. For fixed marginal costs differing across firms, one firm alone must survive. It need not be the one with least marginal cost.

III MONOPOLY SUPPLY SIDE EQILIBRIUM: THE ECONOMY

The economy-wide degree of monopoly is now defined as a weighted average of those across all sectors. In the literature, this aggregation has not been examined in detail nor with care. In particular the individual industry degrees of monopoly are treated as though they were more or less independent of each other. This is unsatisfactory for, as Johnson (1973) has noted, the own price elasticities of demand are mutually dependent as determined by consumer preferences. More specifically there are equalities governing the relations between own- and cross-price elasticities simply because of homogeneity and income constraints on demand functions (see, for instance, Deaton and Muellbauer (1980)). To treat own-price elasticities as independent of each other is to eliminate a potential source of competition since a decrease in an industry's elasticity to increase its degree of monopoly is at the expense of demand and degree of monopoly in other sectors.

Let us explore this problem in more detail by first assuming that each industry is a pure monopoly that demand within each industry depends upon its own price alone (or more restrictively has constant own-price elasticity). Such a demand system is often the one utilised to motivate and explain the theory of the degree of monopoly. It can easily be shown, however, that such a demand system must be generated by a Cobb-Douglas utility function (see Diamond and Mirrlees: 1971). As a result all goods must have unit price elasticity (and zero cross-elasticities). Since revenue is constant for each industry, there would be an incentive to reduce output to an infinitesimal quantity and to raise price indefinitely. The model collapses into nonsense.

If we now retain the same demand system but introduce oligopoly and collusion, the results will be seen to be only a little more palatable. For the sake of argument, assume that each industry has identical firms and number of firms. Then the industry *and* economy degree of monopoly is simply $\alpha + ((1 - \alpha)/n)$ since $e = 1$ and $H = 1/n$. This result demonstrates that the degree of monopoly for the economy is that of the average industry, *independent* of the number of industries in the economy. It is a highly implausible result. An economy with a large number of industries all producing for immediate consumption is as uncompetitive as one with a small number or even one industry. This complements vertically integrated production in which firms pass on the monopoly prices of their inputs together with their own mark-up so that ultimately pricing is independent of the number of firms involved in intermediate production. There would appear to be no competition amongst industries over both final markets and over intermediate production.

These results are contingent on the assumption of the Cobb-Douglas utility function, although this assumption is often implicit in much aggregate monopoly analysis (and a theory which fails for a standard utility function is questionable). As defined, the individual industry degree of monopoly depends, in terms of demand, on own-price elasticity alone. Consequently, the aggregate degree of monopoly depends on some weighted sum of own-price elasticities. In general, there are no restrictions on the sum of one-price elasticities although they are mutually conditioned with cross-elasticities since, in terms of inverse elasticities:

$$e_i = -e_{ii} = \sum_{j \neq 1} \frac{e_{ji}w_k}{w_i} \quad \text{where} \quad e_{ji} = \frac{\partial p_j}{\partial X_i} \cdot \frac{X_i}{p_j}$$

and w_j is the budget share of the jth good.

Assume that zero cross elasticities are implausible to get away from the implications of the Cobb-Douglas utility function. The demand in each industry depends on all prices, and the monopolist presumably recognises this. From the equation above, the degree of monopoly can be seen to depend on own-price elasticity in a way which is equivalent to taking a weighted sum of all cross-price elasticities. These cross-elasticities measure substitution and hence competition between industries in the economy. It is because these cross elasticities were zero for Cobb-Douglas utility functions that the degree of monopoly became so implausibly high and independent of the number of industries for oligopoly. In this more general case, it can be seen that the degree of monopoly is increased through increasing e_i only by increasing one or more of e_{ji} ($j \neq i$), that is by decreasing substitution between goods. For the economy as a whole, it is simply misleading to consider that the degree of monopoly can be increased by decreasing own-price elasticities as if these were independent of other sectors. Rather, the degree of monopoly is determined by the degree of substitution between goods. As before, this raises problems of whether the degree of monopoly decreases with the number of industries, as might be expected. There are more goods, increasing the potential for substitution, but equally substitution between existing goods is liable to be reduced by the presence of the new. Quite apart from this, to assume that the economy degree of monopoly can be increased by reducing own-price elasticities is equivalent, not surprisingly, simply to assuming away competition for demand between sectors.

It could be argued that industries can increase the degree of monopoly by acting in concert to reduce subsitution between goods. This raises a second problem once industry demand is no longer taken to depend on own price alone: to what extent does an industry take account of the non-competitive behaviour and general equilibrium effects that result from its own output choice? Some other industries may welcome an output expansion if complementary to their own products whilst others may retaliate in some way in contrast to the intra-industry situation in which goods are the closest of substitutes. Only if all goods are gross substitutes can it be presumed that collusion is general and reinforcing to reduce cross-elasticities. This condition of gross substitutes would also be sufficient (and no satisfactory weaker necessary condition has been found) for two further properties. The first is that the oligopoly equilibrium (or more exactly the perfectly competitive equilibrium from which it departs) should be stable and unique. Second, without this condition there is the possibility of "perverse" price effects. An industry may increase its degree of collusion and hence monopoly only to find that this results in a decrease in profitability when it works through the system because of associated shifts in its own demand curve. Without gross substitutes, it is possible that *ceteris paribus*, an exogenous shift in demand towards a product may result in its price decreasing.[1] As an increase in the degree of collusion can be seen as equivalent to a shift in demand, it follows that an increase in degree of monopoly may decrease profitability. In a more direct way, for example, by increasing price, oligopolists may increase the cost of their own consumption more than the profits that accrue from the degree of monopoly.[2] This is a specific example of a more general problem of the neoclassical theory of monopoly in a general equilibrium framework. How far do agents take account of their decisions in the absence of perfect competition? The condition of gross substitutes which does away with these problems of perverse prices, stability, uniqueness and interindustry collusion is, however, precisely the one which suggests a low degree of monopoly.

IV COMPARATIVE STATICS

In the previous section, we have established that the equilibrium associated with a colluding industry depends on the degree of collusion, α, and the given demand and cost curves. For simplicity, we assume in this section that the elasticity of demand is constant and that the same applies to each individual firm's marginal cost.

From (4)

$$X_i(1 - \alpha)\frac{dp}{dX} = c_i - p - \alpha X\frac{dp}{dX}.$$

Aggregating

$$X(1 - \alpha)\frac{dp}{dX} = nc - np - n\alpha X\frac{dp}{dX} \quad \text{where} \quad nc = C = \sum c_i$$

so that c is the simple average marginal cost across the industry.

$$X\frac{dp}{dX}(1 - \alpha + n\alpha) = C - np$$

$$n - e(1 - \alpha + n\alpha) = \frac{C}{p}$$

Hence

(8)
$$p = \frac{C}{n - e(1 - \alpha + n\alpha)}$$

This formula yields the monopoly price in terms of the parameters of the system (including the number of firms which we have not explicitly considered before). As a result, there is an implied level of industry output, depending on the position of the constant-elasticity demand curve. From this, the firm by firm output is deducible from the equation.

(9)
$$\frac{X_i}{X} = \frac{p(1 - \alpha e) - c_i}{(1 - \alpha)ep}$$

which is immediate from the first equation given in this section.

Comparative statics results for the industry are immediate.

(i) if c_i increases, so does C and p and hence there is a decline in X.

(ii) If n increases p declines since $1 - \alpha e > 0$ and there is an increase in X (as long as firms enter on average with marginal cost c, otherwise C is also affected).

(iii) If α increases, p increases and X declines.

(iv) If e increases (or demand is more inelastic), p increases and X declines.

These are more or less what would be expected intuitively. In addition, it can be seen that price only depends linearly on the sum of marginal costs. Results of changes in the parameters for individual firms are not quite so easily obtained. From (9)

$$\frac{X_i}{X_j} = \frac{p(1 - \alpha e) - c_i}{p(1 - \alpha e) - c_j}$$

$$= 1 + \frac{c_j - c_i}{p(1 - \alpha e) - c_j}$$

Assume w.l.o.g. that $c_j > c_i$. Then $X_i > X_j$ as would be expected. If n increases (with average cost c remaining the same) then p falls and relative market shares widen even though the effect of this is to reduce each firm's share (see 9)). For changes in α (and e) there is a direct effect which is to widen dispersion and an indirect effect through p which is to reduce it since p increases.

$$\frac{\partial \left(\frac{X_i}{X_j}\right)}{\partial \alpha} \gtreqless 0 \quad \text{as} \quad \frac{\partial p}{\partial \alpha}(1 - \alpha e) - ep \lesseqgtr 0$$

$$\text{as} \quad ep - \frac{(1 - \alpha e)pe(n - 1)}{n - e(1 - \alpha + n\alpha)} \gtreqless 0$$

$$\text{as} \quad n - e + e\alpha - ne\alpha - n + 1 + \alpha en - \alpha e \gtreqless 0$$

$$\text{as} \quad 1 - e \gtreqless 0$$

It follows that an increase in collusion increases dispersion of market shares since $e < 1$ and it might be felt that this renders increased collusion difficult to achieve.

$$\frac{\partial\left(\frac{X_i}{X_j}\right)}{\partial e} \gtreqless 0 \quad \text{as} \quad \frac{\partial p}{\partial e}(1 - \alpha e) - p\alpha < 0.$$

$$\text{as} \quad \alpha p - \frac{(1 - \alpha e)p(1 - \alpha + n\alpha)}{n - e(1 - \alpha + n\alpha)} \gtreqless 0$$

$$\text{as} \quad \alpha n - \alpha e + \alpha^2 e - \alpha^2 ne - 1 + \alpha - n\alpha + \alpha e - \alpha^2 e + \alpha^2 ne \gtreqless 0.$$

$$\text{as} \quad -1 + \alpha \gtreqless 0.$$

It follows that an increase in e (decrease in elasticity) has the effect of reducing dispersion of market shares so that firms have a greater incentive for collusion through increasing e (eg by collective advertising) than through raising α directly.

We have already argued that market shares are determined by the distribution of marginal costs. This can be presented most simply as follows. From (9)

$$\frac{X_i}{X} = \frac{1 - \alpha e}{(1 - \alpha)e} - \frac{c_i}{(1 - \alpha)ep}.$$

Substituting for p and subtracting $1/n$ from both sides

$$\frac{X_i}{X} - \frac{1}{n} = \frac{1 - \alpha e}{(1 - \alpha)e} - \frac{1}{n} - \frac{c_i}{nc}\frac{(n(1 - \alpha e) - (1 - \alpha)e)}{(1 - \alpha)e}$$

$$= \frac{1 - \alpha e}{(1 - \alpha)e} - \frac{1}{n} - \frac{c_i}{c}\left(\frac{1 - \alpha e}{(1 - \alpha)e} - \frac{1}{n}\right).$$

$$(10) \quad \frac{X_i}{X} - \frac{1}{n} = A\left(1 - \frac{c_i}{c}\right).$$

where

$$A = \frac{1 - \alpha e}{(1 - \alpha)e} - \frac{1}{n}.$$

This demonstrates that the divergence of market shares from their mean $(1/n)$ is identically, but inversely, distributed to the divergence of relative marginal costs from their mean. A corollary is that a firm with average marginal cost has an average market share. Casual empirical observation might cast doubt on these theoretical conclusions. Market shares seem highly dispersed compared to the distribution of market costs.

V STABILITY

In the previous section we examined conditions governing equilibrium in oligopolistic industries. Here we intend to consider the stability of equilibrium. Consider first the economy as a whole. In so far as the monopolised economy is an equilibrium departure from the perfectly competitive outcome, it is plausible to suggest that a necessary condition for stability is that the perfectly competitive outcome be stable. As the only general sufficient condition known for this is that all goods be gross substitutes, this is again extremely restrictive.

It is, however, possible that the exercise of monopoly power will have the effect of stabilising the otherwise unstable competitive economy. This clearly depends on the mechanism of adjustment. We intend to examine this at the level of the industry in a way that conforms with the method by which equilibrium has itself been established. Alternatively, this stability analysis can be interpreted in terms merely of the rationality of each firm's conjectures about the others' behaviour.

Here we meet with a problem. Each firm is presumed to maximise profits contingent upon retaliatory behaviour. It seems sensible to analyse stability on the basis that the expected retaliatory behaviour is in fact realised. This, however, gives two forms of firm behaviour. On the one hand, there is profit maximisation but there is also punitive retaliation which will in general diverge from profit maximisation.

A further problem involves the interpretation of the degree of collusion α. There are two possibilities. The simplest is that when one firm increases output, all the others respond by increasing their own output in the proportion α to their market shares and then no subsequent retaliatory action is taken. That further retaliatory action might be taken follows from the punitive measures consequent upon those already made. We return to this second case later. For the moment, we observe that the result of the once and for all retaliatory action is an increase in output of

$$1 + \frac{\alpha(X_k - X_{ik})}{X_k}$$

where the ith firm initially increases its output by 1. This is the new equilibrium until retaliatory behaviour is abandoned and there is a return to profit-maximising behaviour. Clearly, the result is stable. We shall refer to this case as *formal* collusion. It is characterised by the retaliatory firms acting in concert with each other, that is without retaliating against each other in response to their own punitive increase in output. In some ways the situation is comparable to a Stackelberg oligopoly. One firm leads by increasing its output whilst anticipating retaliatory action by all other firms at the rate α, whilst the other firms do indeed behave in this way. If retaliatory behaviour were replaced by profit maximisation, the result would be a Stackelberg oligopoly.

Alternatively we have the case of *informal* collusion. Here firms simply adopt the behaviour rate of retaliating at the rate α whenever other firms increase their output. This has an affinity with the behaviour associated with Cournot oligopoly. Each firm behaves as if each others firm's output is given. If the behaviour were profit maximisation or if α were zero, the result would be the Cournot solution.

For both formal and informal collusion the equilibrium conditions given by equation (4) are the same since each firm behaves as if output increase will be $X_{ik} + \alpha(X_k - X_{ik})$. In case of formal collusion, firms act to hold output at this level. The situation for informal collusion is entirely different as it generates a spiral of retaliatory behaviour. Each firm responds to the retaliatory behaviour of other firms and so on. It can be shown that the recursive increase in output created is finite if and only if $\alpha(n - 1) < 1$. This is easily seen for symmetric market shares. For then, any unit increase in output induces each firm to increase its own output by an amount α except to the extent that it is responsible for the initial increase in output. This means overall that $(n-1)\alpha$ must be the industry increase in output since on average $(n-1)$ firms have responded at rate α to the output increase. For an initial increase in output of unity by one firm, the subsequent industry response is period by period $(n-1)\alpha$, $(n-1)^2\alpha^2$, $(n-1)^3\alpha^3$, ... [3] This sums to a finite amount as long as $(n-1)\alpha < 1$. In the appendix, we demonstrate that the same condition is necessary for stability irrespective of the initial distribution of market shares and output increases across firms.

This result calls for some interpretation. It suggests that cumulative retaliatory action leads to an infinite expansion of industry output if $(n-1)\alpha \geqslant 1$. This may not happen in practice since there will presumably be some return to profit-maximising behaviour before profits are entirely eroded. Nevertheless, the informal collusion cannot rely on punitive action to work itself out prior to a return to the equilibrium and in this sense the equilibrium is unstable.

The condition $(n-1)\alpha < 1$ is open to a natural interpretation. If $(n-1)\alpha \geqslant 1$ then the industry is an unstable oligopoly and cannot be presumed to survive. On the other hand, if $(n-1)\alpha < 1$, this suggests that the industry is colluding more than is necessary to maintain an oligopoly.

It follows that $(n-1)\alpha = 1$ is the relationship between n and α specifying the boundary for informal collusion. We might even term it the law of informal collusion. As is generally recognised, an inverse relationship is liable to exist between α and n irrespective of the form of collusion, $(n-1)\alpha = 1$ is an exact specification of the boundary of this relationship for informal collusion, for firms acting spontaneously to restrict output and raise prices.

As an exercise, let us presume that we have an industry characterised by such an informal collusion and also by equal market shares.

$$\mu = e\left(\alpha + \frac{(1-\alpha)}{n}\right) = \frac{e}{n}\left((n-1)\alpha + 1\right) = \frac{2e}{n}.$$

This suggests that the degree of monopoly itself decreases quite rapidly as the number of firms in the industry increases.[4]

APPENDIX: STABILITY OF RETALIATORY OLIGOPOLY

We assume that the percentage relation α is in proportion to market shares in equilibrium and that α does not vary as these shares change (as they do as a result of initial output increase and retaliation). Let $y^t = (y_1^t, y_2^t, \ldots, y_n^t)$ be the column vector of retaliations by firms at time t where y_i refers to the ith firm. Then $y^{t+1} = \alpha X y^t$ where X is the matrix (X_{ij}) where $X_{ij} = 0$ if $i = j$ and $X_{ij} = X_i/X_j$ if $i \neq j$, X_i being the output of the ith firm in equilibrium. That is:

$$y_1^{t+1} = 0 + \alpha \frac{X_1}{X_2} y_2^t + \alpha \frac{X_1}{X_2} y_3^t + \ldots + \alpha \frac{X_1}{X_2} y_n^t.$$

The stability of the oligopoly can then be seen to depend on the properties of the matrix αX since $y^t = \alpha^t X^t y^0$.

We state without proof that the matrix X has characteristic equation for its eigenvalues given by $(\lambda + \alpha)^{n-1}(\lambda - (n-1)\alpha) = 0$ since $\alpha < 1$ except for perfect colluion, it follows that stability depends upon $(n-1)\alpha < 1$.

We approach this problem more indirectly to give a flavour of the results (which will be seen to correspond to the coincidence of $(n-1)$ of the eigenvalues). Suppose the ith firm increases output by a unit quantity, then each firm $j \neq i$ responds by increasing output by $\alpha(X_j/X_i)$ and i's response is to increase output no further until the following period.

Lemma y_i^i may be written as A_t and y_j^i as $B_t(X_j/X_i)$ for $i \neq j$ where A_t and B_t are independent of firm outputs $X_i, \ldots, X_n$.

Proof By induction. Clearly true for $t = 0$. Assume true for t.

$$y_{t+1}^i = \sum_{j \neq 1} B_t \cdot \frac{X_j}{X_i} \cdot \frac{X_i}{X_j} \alpha = (n-1)\alpha B_t = A_{t+1}$$

which is independent of $X_1, \ldots, X_n$

$$y_{t+1}^i = \sum_{r \neq i,j} B_t \frac{X_r}{X_i} \cdot \frac{X_j}{X_r} \alpha + \alpha A_t \frac{X_j}{X_i}$$

$$= (n-2)\alpha B_t \frac{X_j}{X_i} + \alpha A_t \frac{X_j}{X_i}$$

$$= B_{t+1} \frac{X_j}{X_i}$$

where B_{t+1} is independent of $X_1, \ldots, X_n$.

Q.E.D.

Now

$$A_{t+1} = (n-1)\alpha B_t$$

$$B_{t+1} = (n-2)\alpha B_t + \alpha A_t$$

$$B_{t+1} = (n-2)\alpha B_t(n-1)\alpha^2 B_{t-1} = 0$$

This has auxiliary equation

$$x^2 - (n-2)\alpha x - (n-1)\alpha^2 = 0.$$

$$(x - (n-1)\alpha)(x + \alpha) = 0$$

$$B_t = a(n-1)^t\alpha^t + b(-\alpha)^t \text{ for constants a and b}$$

$$A_t = a(n-1)^t\alpha^t + b(-\alpha)^{t-1}(n-1)\alpha$$

$$= a(n-1)^t\alpha^t - b(-\alpha)^t(n-1).$$

Initially $A_t = 1$, $B_t = 0$.

$$a + b = 0$$

$$a - b(n-1) = 1.$$

Hence $a = -b = 1/n$.

$$A_t = \frac{\alpha^t(n-1)((n-1)^{t-1} + (-1)^t)}{n}$$

$$B_t = \frac{\alpha^t((n-1)^t - (-1)^t)}{n}$$

Increase in industry output at time t is

$$A_t + \sum_{j \neq i} B_t \frac{X_j}{X_i} = A_t + B_t \frac{(X - X_i)}{X_i}$$

where $X = \Sigma X_j$. By inspection, we see that this depends on geometric progressions in $\alpha(n-1)$ and $(-\alpha)$. Consequently, increase in output converges if and only if $\alpha(n-1) < 1$.

This result is true for all i and consequently for any linear combination of initial increases in output distributed across the firms.

NOTES

1. See Brown (1982) for an extended discussion of such perverse prices in the context of the neoclassical concept of scarcity.
2. This raises the question of conjectural equilibrium which we do not consider in detail; see Gollop and Roberts (1979), for example.
3. In the first period firm i raises output by one unit. The remaining $(n - 1)$ firms raise output by α, and so their overall response is $(n - 1)\alpha$. In the third period, the original firm i raises output by $\alpha(n - 1)\alpha$, and the remaining $(n - 2)$ firms each raise output by $(n - 1)\alpha$. So in the third period we have $(n - 1)(\alpha)(n - 1)(\alpha)$ which gives $(n - 1)^2\alpha^2$, and so the series progresses.
4. A key paper in the definition of price—cost margins is Clarke and Davies (1980).

5 Monopoly Supply Side Economics: An Informal Analysis

I THE BASIC MODEL

From the side of production, or more exactly supply, a central role is played by the theory of oligopoly in Cowling's (1982) analysis.[1] In particular, there is a focus on the degree of monopoly as first defined by Kalecki (1971), but see also Lerner (1934) and, more recently, Reynolds (1983). Leaving aside oligopoly and considering monopoly alone for the moment, this theory is based on the simple notion that an industry will push up price and reduce output to increase profits. It is better able to do so the more inelastic is demand since output and revenue can be maintained despite relatively large price increases. This concept of the effect of monopoly is far from new. Indeed, it appears to have a lineage as long as markets themselves have existed.[2] In general, the effect of monopolies has been condemned as against the "public interest" and so the criticism of monopolies on this basis is no radical point of departure.

Where the Kalecki tradition has introduced some considerable novelty is in generalising the monopoly effect to the economy as a whole or at least to its dominant part. Associated with this is the notion that the "public interest" harmed by monopoly is consumption as the ultimate goal of economic activity and this is readily identified with the standard of living of the working class. As it were, the ultimate effect of monopoly, industry by industry, is to reduce the level of real wages, below what they would otherwise have been in the absence of monopoly, through pushing up the relative price of consumption goods.

At first sight there is little to distinguish this view from the orthodox neoclassical theory of the deadweight loss to be associated with monopoly. The departure from competitive equilibrium is Pareto inefficient with consumers more than losing the extra profits that have been pocketed by a monopoly. The partial equilibrium of conventional monopoly theory has been generalised to the economy as a whole and consumption has been predominantly identified with the working class.

At second sight, this affinity between neoclassical economics and the Kaleckian tradition is *confirmed*. Each industry is presumed to be identified with a single product with a uniform price. The industry faces a fixed demand curve. Within each industry, each of a (small) number of firms is presumed to maximise profits subject to given but not necessarily identical cost functions.[3] In contrast to perfect competition, each firm maximises profits, taking account of two factors. First, its own expansion of output increases industry output and reduces price. Second, any increase in its own output may be subject to a penalising increase in output from competitors. The more this is liable to be so, the more hesitant firms are to increase output and the more the industry acts like a monopoly. Consequently the greater the fear of reprisals, the more firms within an industry appear to collude and this is represented formally by a degree of collusion designated by α. For $\alpha = 1$, the industry enjoys perfect collusion which is equivalent to monopoly. For $\alpha = 0$, each firm takes account only of its own output on the industry price level in contrast to perfect competition where it is oblivious even of this. The situation in which $\alpha = 0$ is known as the Cournot solution. Cournot and pure monopoly are seen by Cowling as the two extremes within which an industry must fall.

It is worth pausing at this stage to observe that the basic unit of analysis is the individual firm. Aggregating over these within an industry yields corresponding price and output for the industry. The mode of analysis is identical to neoclassical economics. Subsequently, there will be an aggregation across industries which have themselves been built up from their constituent firms. This serves as a method of describing the theory; it is not in itself an explicit criticism. Nevertheless, the degree of monopoly is defined as the difference between price and marginal costs as a percentage of price (see Lerner: 1934). By doing this, the theory takes as its standard of comparison the degree of departure from competitive equilibrium, for which price and marginal cost are equal. Embodied within each oligopolistic industry is a perfectly competitive one which remains an organising concept to measure the degree of monopoly, if not to characterise the state of equilibrium itself. The same applies to the economy as a whole.

In the previous chapter, the plausible result was shown that market shares within an industry are distributed across firms in inverse proportion to their marginal costs.[4] This simple result has important implications. First, it suggests that the assumption of given cost functions is extremely restrictive or, more exactly, that this eliminates an important source of competition, since firms could attempt to increase individual market shares by investing or whatever to decrease marginal costs.[4] Second, it suggests that the notion of collusion employed is extremely restrictive, since production costs for the industry could be reduced by redistributing production towards those firms with lower marginal costs. Third, there is the relationship between these two factors. The first implies a tendency towards equal market shares through competition to reduce marginal costs, whilst the second implies a tendency towards dispersion of market shares as firms collude to diminish costs in the industry on the basis of unequal marginal costs. This suggests that the problem of oligopoly is not best analysed as an equilibrium divergence from perfect competition since, even then, it contains within it the forces for a breach of those equilibrium conditions, whether by changes in cost functions or redistribution of market shares.

Finally, it must be observed that there is no explanation of the initial distribution of cost functions, and this is not unrelated to the previous points. In so far as the distribution of costs has been taken as the given result of some historical process, one which is presumably competitive, there is no reason to bring this process of competition to an abrupt halt in order to allow an oligopolistic equilibrium to be defined.[5]

Since the characteristics of that equilibrium are determined by the distribution of costs, it is the explanation of these that is most important, but most notably absent.[6]

Leaving these problems aside and aggregating over the industry, it has been shown that the degree of monopoly for the industry is given by $e(\alpha + (1 - \alpha)H)$ here e is the inverse of the elasticity of demand and H is the Herfindahl index, a measure of market concentration that varies between $1/n$ and 1 where n is the number of firms. H takes on the lower value if shares are equal and rises to unity when one firm accounts for all output. This formula for the degree of monopoly can be misleading, since it can give the impression that the degree of monopoly is *determined* by e, α and H as exogenous or mutually conditioning parameters. In fact, only α together with the cost functions, the demand function (which may have a constant elasticity) and the number of firms are exogenous. H (and e) are *determined by these*. In other words, it does not make sense to say that the degree of monopoly is greater because H is greater. The point is best illustrated by an analogy. Revenue for an industry equals price multiplied by quantity. This is how it is *calculated*. But it is not *determined* by price and quantity as if the two were independent.

From this discussion and from the formula for the degree of monopoly, it follows that the difference between firms is of limited conceptual significance in this model. Differences are confined to those of cost and these determine the distribution of output across the industry, by which the measure of market concentration is formed. This in turn influences the overall degree of monopoly and, in this sense, differences in costs have a quantitative effect. But the most significant and causal factor, the originally formed distribution of costs, remains unexplained and, as a determining process by which firms differentiate themselves on the basis of cost, it is absent from the analysis, even though the resulting cost functions are so basic. It is in this sense that it makes little difference whether firms are identical or not since the process by which they change is absent. As already observed, this eliminates the process of competition between firms at the level of costs and confines attention to the extent to which competition is minimised at the level of the market through collusion. This entails a rigid separation between cost and price competition, with the elimination of the former and its effects on the latter. Accordingly, an industry acts as if it were a single firm that does not exploit its monopoly position fully.

In this light, little of substance is lost if we treat each firm as identical. It also has the advantage of easing exposition. In this case, each firm has the same market share and H takes on the value $1/n$. The degree of monopoly becomes $e(\alpha + (1 - \alpha/n))$.[7]

We now have a number of industries confronting each other, each with a degree of monopoly as already described. The standard procedure is to take a weighted average of the industries to obtain an overall degree of monopoly for the economy as a whole, the monopoly power with which producers (capital) confront consumers (workers). In the literature, this aggregation across industries has not been conducted very carefully. Implicitly, it has been presumed that demand within each sector is independent of demand in other sectors—as if there is no competition between sectors for markets in the sense that the demand for each good depends on its own price alone. It can be shown mathematically that this is so if and only if each elasticity of demand within a sector is unity. This has the implication of constant revenue for each industry irrespective of the quantity sold. Higher prices just compensate lower sales and vice versa as far as revenue is concerned. Each industry would have an incentive to reduce output to an infinitesimally small quantity and raise price enormously since revenue is constant. Such a demand system would have a degree of monopoly μ for the whole economy equal to $\alpha + (1 - \alpha/n)$ since e equals unity for every industry, where n is the typical number of firms in an industry.

This result does not appear to have been explicitly recognised in the literature. It has one profound implication: that the degree of monopoly is that of the average industry independent of the number of industries in the economy. An economy with one hundred industries each with the same degree of monopoly has an overall level of monopoly that is the same as an economy with a single industry with that degree of monopoly. This is intuitively implausible and with good reason. It highlights the absence of competition between industries for resources, including labour, and for markets in which to sell. The economy is simply a number of vertically integrated production processes in which firms pass on a monopoly markup on their costs. It makes no difference vertically where one industry begins and another ends, since even capitalists making purchases as inputs are powerless against the degree of monopoly possessed by suppliers. There is also no effective competition between sectors serving final demand.[8]

The preceding paragraphs apply only for a system in which demand depends on own price alone. It does demonstrate the dangers of aggregating over sectors as if they were independent. More generally, no exact result can be obtained for the average price elasticity of demand.[9] For a more general system a decrease in an own-price elasticity of demand must be at the expense of cross-elasticities (or demand in other sectors). In other words, for the economy as a whole, the aggregate degree of monopoly can be increased through manipulation of demand (to decrease own-price elasticities) only by decreasing cross-elasticities on aggregate, which is itself equivalent to reducing competition between sectors for final demand. Whilst it might appear that the degree of monopoly can be simply increased by decreasing own-price elasticity, for the economy as a whole this is a more or less tautological result. For decreases in own-price elasticity are equivalent to decreases in substitution whilst no explanation is given of why this should be so.[10]

The results concerning the aggregation of the elasticities of demand is interesting in the light of previous discussions of this point. Johnson (1973) argues that labour's share cannot be explained in the economy as a whole in terms of the degree of monopoly (and the inverse of the elasticity of demand)

the elasticity of demand is not determined by the capitalists in a particular industry, since it is not a parameter of behaviour but a variable, and the precise value of it at the profit-maximising point is determined by profit maximisation by entrepreneurs, while the underlying behaviour determining the demand expressed in the market for products is a matter of consumer preferences not of monopolistic firm behaviour.

Johnson (1973) p. 198

Johnson is acutely aware that the patterns of demand are interrelated in such a way that the expansion of expenditure in one sector must be at the expense of others. Cowling's (1982) retort to this is that:

the degree of monopoly is determined by concentration and the degree of collusion, as well as by the elasticity of demand, but also, the elasticity of demand is itself at least partly a variable within the control of the firms in question, just as the degree of concentration and collusion are.

Cowling (1982) p. 10

Thus, for Johnson, μ is determined by consumer preferences and the elasticity of demand is of vital importance at the sectoral level but outside the direct control of capitalists within that sector. It is not clear that Johnson is aware that on average the configuration of consumer preferences may have no effect at all on the degree of monopoly in the economy as a whole despite the interdependence between own and cross-elasticities. For Cowling, μ is determined by H and α as well as by e at the level of each individual sector and consequently for the economy as a whole. This contradicts the basic logic for his model, since e and H are determined endogenously by the exogenously given α and cost and demand functions. If e and H are to be related with each other and other factors, then it becomes illegitimate to use the derived formula for the degree of concentration to analyse the effects of such additional influences, since the formula has been obtained in the absence of their mutual conditioning. Thus, whilst it can be suggested that a high elasticity in a sector might induce a greater degree of collusion, this cannot be applied to the formula for the degree of monopoly which is based on the assumption that α is exogenous and e is not. For, if these added relationships do exist, it must be presumed that firms recognise them and adjust their behaviour and the formula for the degree of monopoly accordingly.[11]

II OTHER CONSIDERATIONS

In modifying the account of the formulation of the degree of monopoly, Cowling and others have placed great emphasis on the role played by advertising as a means of decreasing elasticity. But can this argument be generalised to the economy as a whole? Does advertising increase the degree of monopoly by decreasing elasticities sector by sector? As we have presented the issue the answer is not straightforward. The sum of elasticities of demand is not fixed. Nevertheless, advertising is competitive across sectors and cannot necessarily decrease the sum of elasticities, even if one sector or one firm can gain at the expense of another. It is not clear that advertising is directed towards reducing substitution between goods in aggregate.

However, the issue is more complicated since it depends on over which sectors of the economy the aggregation of elasticities takes place. The degree of monopoly is defined relative to the markets for goods and services, but it could be argued that elasticities there could be reduced by reducing saving and leisure (increasing the elasticity of demand for these). We deal with each in turn. For saving, there are profit-maximising and other institutions which advertise heavily to influence consumer preferences. On the face of it, there is no reason to presume that advertising for saving should be any less elasticity shifting than for other goods and services. Even so, the argument would depend on an upward shift in the working-class propensity to consume. This is not the place to rehearse the literature concerning the consumption function. Certainly the evidence seems to suggest that there are different propensities to consume between groups in society (Murfin (1980) and Arestis and Driver (1980)) and this, taken together with life-cycle behaviour, might suggest that there is little room for workers to increase consumption significantly, whatever the net quantity of non-competitive advertising expenditure. The position of Marglin (1974) that the workers' propensity to consume is already unity seems most plausible. For, otherwise, we would be witnessing an increase in the wealth of capital stock owned by the working class.[12] There seems little evidence of that. In short, after the effects of advertising to encourage saving, the already high propensities to consume and the redistribution of expenditure to earlier points in the life-cycle, there is little room left for a permanent increase in the degree of monopoly through an advertising-induced reduction in demand elasticities.

The second effect is that focused upon by Brack and Cowling (1980): the positive impact of advertising on labour supply. It is argued that advertising encourages workers to work longer hours so that they may obtain more income as a means to acquire more goods. Here we are in the terrain of labour-supply curves, which like consumption functions, are liable to remain controversial. We merely observe that the argument introduces (workers') income through labour supply into the analysis for the first time. Having done so, this suggests that the conditions of optimisation might themselves be modified quite apart from the parameters of the system. Moreover, there is an increased demand because workers have been employed more and have *produced* more. In fact, they must produce more than they demand to leave way for profits (as well as advertising expenditure). Since, within the Kaleckian macroenomic tradition, consumption out of profits is low, the net effect of advertising through labour suply could be to reduce aggregate demand relative to aggregate supply and the degree of monopoly with it.

The discussion of the demand system as a whole raises other problems, ones which highlight the absence of certain aspects of competition. There is a neglect of upstream-downstream bargaining and of vertical integration to secure supply advantages. Galbraith's position on this warrants some discussion. He argues that the decline of competition among sellers (i.e. increasing concentration) has brought into existence strong buyers. The existence of market power "creates an incentive to the organisation of another position of power that neutralises it" (Galbraith (1963) pp. 125–6). Thus, where buyers are concentrated, we should expect the ability of oligopolistic sellers to charge a price above marginal cost to be reduced (see also Lustgarten: 1975). However, recent papers by Waterson (1980) and (1982) appear to turn Galbraith's analysis on its head. Waterson looks at the impact on an industry's price-cost margin of firms in downstream industries having seller market power. His theoretical model predicts that margins are, in fact, increased by an increase in successive market power of this type. He finds that there are two opposing effects: increased concentration in the buyer industry raises the total margin open to the buyer and seller industry but reduces the seller industry's share of this margin, and the net effect is to increase the seller industry's margin. (Empirically, he finds that for the UK the successive market-power effect outweighs the Galbraith-type effect.) Thus, we can see that the Kaleckian view of collusion can be extended to vertical as well as horizontal relations between firms.

Nevertheless, Waterson's analysis remains within a partial equilibrium framework. It requires that demand no longer depends on own price alone, and raises the question of collusion across industries. Given that other prices enter into the demand for a firm's product, then the firm should take account of retaliation from firms in other industries in response to its own price changes. These come in two forms. First, other industries act as buyers and respond unfavourably to price increases, in contrast to firms within the industry concerned. Second, other firms also sell and will respond unfavourably to price increases which absorb revenue at elasticities less than one, although demand will tend to shift favourably also (income and substitution effects, respectively). The sum effect for the economy as a whole depends on how retaliatory behaviour is modelled. But given the identities that connect (cross) price and income elasticities, it cannot be presumed that the results of partial equilibrium can be taken as representative of the economy as a whole.

Within Cowling's analysis, retaliatory behaviour is understood entirely in terms of the value of α, the degree of collusion:

there are obviously many theories of oligopoly but they simply relate to the value of α.

Cowling (1982) p. 35

One result of this is that the pattern of *ownership* within the industry is insignificant. For example, for perfect collusion, $\alpha = 1$, we have the case of pure monopoly even though the industry may not be owned as a monopoly. In the absence of pure monopoly the number of firms does become important. Cowling suggests that the number of firms is liable to decrease in pursuit of a greater degree of monopoly, but that the associated increase in profitability does not lead to entry by other firms. He relies here on the arguments of Spence (1977), for whom there is a separation between the problems of pricing within the industry and the raising of barriers to those outside. Essentially, the latter can be realised by excess capacity alone. This threatens increased output and price reductions on potential entrants. Consequently, a low price need not be used to deter entry.

Cowling argues that the use of excess capacity as a barrier to entry is pervasive for monopoly capitalism. It is suggested that at the firm level excess capacity should increase with market share. It was argued above, however, that in this model greater market shares will result from lower marginal costs. Consequently, although firms with smaller market shares and higher marginal costs would have less of an incentive and need to protect lower monopoly profits, they are at a greater competitive risk from entry than larger firms. It is implausible that firms with such relatively high costs would invest in excess capacity to protect a relatively weak degree of monopoly rather than to reduce those high costs. That the existence of excess capacity makes for both greater collusion and conflict over market shares, is recognised, although the former is emphasised. If there is greater collusion as a result of excess capacity individually constructed to deter entrants, then the industry could collude over the excess capacity to be provided. This weakens the case for the existence of pervasive excess capacity.

Some of this reasoning is heavily, but implicitly, contingent upon the assumption of the irrelevance of patterns of ownership. Entry, for example, is always seen within the standard industrial economics literature as a new firm setting up within the industry at the expense of others. Presumably if it were to buy into the industry, it is supposed to behave exactly the same as the firm it has displaced. In fact, entry by purchase of a firm might appear more attractive if that firm had excess capacity, since aggressive intentions could be realised immediately. This might not alter the number of firms within the industry but it casts continuing doubts on the efficacy of collusion and of excess capacity as a deterrent to entry.

To summarise, on the supply side, the model that Cowling develops contains several weaknesses, and those weaknesses are systematically related to a one-sided view of the relation-ship between monopolisation and competition. This view recognises the potential for conflict and cooperation within monopolised markets but places more emphasis on the effects of cooperation (the degree of collusion α) and its association with output restriction, high prices and, as we will see, stagnation. In contrast, we have found—by develop-ing the Kaleckian model of the degree of monopoly, even on the grounds of its own assumptions—that the results pro-duced tend to expose for rejection those very assumptions on which the theory is based. For example, that market shares are distributed in a simple relationship to firms' costs renders unsatisfactory the assumption that firms will not invest and compete to reduce costs. The same considerations apply to other factors such as excess capacity and manipulation of demand curves. It is only by excluding by assumption the effects of competition within an economy with monopolised markets that the theory, not surprisingly, yields the results that it does.

Now one response to this would be to incorporate more general assumptions within the models used, to take account of the factors that have been seen to be absent. This would not be a fruitful approach for a number of reasons. At the level of theory itself, quite apart from mathematical tract-ability, the result would simply be to specify with more detail and variety the influences on individual firm behaviour, whether these are internal or external to the firm (choice of cost function or negotiation of degree of collusion, respect-ively, for example). In doing so, it is apparent that the conse-quent equilibrium obtained will be moved in one direction or another along the line joining an economy of pure monopolies at one extreme as opposed to an economy of perfect competition at the other. The beauty of the Cowling model is that it is already capable of this in its simplest form, with pure monopoly given by α or n equal to 1 and perfect competition given by $\alpha = 0$ and $n \to \infty$ (or alternatively $\alpha = -1$). What is at stake is not the introduction of more complicating factors that vary the position that the economy occupies upon this line joining perfect competition to perfect monopoly. It is the very idea that such a line contains within it the capacity to analyse monopoly capitalism. It is unable to do so because the two extremes that it contains are ideal constructs. Most significantly, in understanding the Kaleckian model in this way, it can be seen that there always remains a simple dichotomy and inverse relation between competition and monopoly although this may be mediated by many factors. In contrast, we would argue that monopoly and competition are inextricably connected and it is fallacious to construct a theory in which one varies in inverse proportion to the other. To some extent this has already been demonstrated by a diagnosis of the internal workings of the Cowling model. The cure for the symptoms discovered by that diagnosis require, however, a radical rupture with the assumptions of that model and we take this up in Chapter 8.

NOTES

1. Cowling makes it clear that he does not analyse production, referring the reader to the work of Braverman (1974) and Friedman (1977). Consequently, supply is treated as an exchange-based category alone; how much to put on the market rather than how to obtain it through production. Whether this analytical dichotomy is acceptable, in particular whether supply can legitimately be isolated from production, is never questioned. Yet it is a major proposition of Marxism that exchange-based categories can only be understood adequately on the basis of the analysis of production relations. The failure of orthodox economics to analyse production is one of its major deficiencies, from a Marxist perspective.

2. See DeRoover (1951) who traces pre-capitalist concepts of monopoly back as far as Aristotle's "Politics".

3. It is presumed that costs include fixed overheads and variable costs each of which may differ across firms.

4. Firms would seek to reduce marginal costs and average fixed costs. Although the latter do not enter directly into the profit-maximisation

conditions, they are crucial in defining the level of profitability at the maximum. In neoclassical terms, of course, increased fixed costs may reduce marginal costs and, in this model, increase market share, but this has to be set against the lower level of profitability. Within Marxism, there is no such necessary trade-off between fixed and marginal costs since the individual accumulation of capital is contingent upon the acquisiton of other capitals as well as investment. The competition to do this is constrained by the availability of finance. Increasing fixed capital and output reduces costs overall as well as increasing profitability because of economies of scale. The second-order conditions for profit maximisation for the model of oligopoly ultimately depend on increasing marginal costs.

5. The number of firms in the industry is also left unexplained. We turn to the discussion of entry later.

6. Significantly, perhaps, Cowling discusses changes in costs in terms of "vintages" of technology. Vintage theory tends to view cost changes as a discrete process connected as a series of equilibria. Necessarily, it thereby excludes competition as a process to gain the new vintage first.

7. The polar cases are (i) $\alpha = 0$ for the Cournot solution, (ii) $\alpha = 1$ or $n = 1$ for the case of pure monopoly.

8. This leads Cowling to the paradoxical result that profits are increased the greater the degree of imports. This is modified later in so far as imports compete with domestic production. Imports raise profits because they are simply price costs which can be marked up by the appropriate degree of monopoly. The reverse implication is that exports must have the opposite effect. Otherwise profits could be raised for the world economy simply by dividing the world into more countries thereby raising the total level of imports.

9. It can be shown for a utility function of the form $u = \Sigma a_i x_i^{b_i}$ that all elasticities are greater than one. Consequently, for this class of utility functions (for which $0 < b_i < 1$ to satisfy second-order conditions), industries would have an incentive to collude to charge infinite prices for infinitesimal quantities.

10. The identities connecting price elasticities follow from budget constraints and homogeneity postulates. See Deaton and Muellbauer (1980).

11. This argument is reminiscent of those used to justify rational expectations! Note that only the oligopolistic firms are assumed to be "rational".

12. This issue is complicated by many factors such as notion of capital owned by workers whether in pension funds or otherwise, whether workers have identical propensities to consume out of wage and other income, etc.

6 The Kaldor-Pasinetti Syndrome

In this chapter it is our intention to employ a model, associated with Kaldor (1956) and Pasinetti (1962) and (1974). We do so to examine Keynesian concepts when they are used in conjunction with macroeconomic aggregates defined in class terms. Specifically, account is to be taken of the distribution of income between profits P and wages W in determining saving and investment behaviour. The Kaldor-Pasinetti model's origins lie in Kaldor's contribution in which he suggested that the level of saving in the economy could adjust to the level of investment by a redistribution of income between profits and wages. Rejecting a uniform rate of saving out of income, typical of the simplest Keynesian models, Kaldor argued that workers and capitalists had different saving rates out of wages and profits, respectively. With capitalists having a higher propensity to save than workers, the saving rate for the economy increases if profits rise at the expense of wages and vice-versa if profits fall.

$$s = s_w \frac{W}{Y} + s_p \frac{P}{Y}$$

$$= (1 - \gamma)s_w + \gamma s_p$$

where s, s_w and s_p are the saving rates for the economy, workers and capitalists, respectively; Y is the level of national income and γ is the share of profits in national income.

As long as the share of investment lies between s_p and s_w, s can adjust so that saving is equal to investment. The circumstances in which this occurs is open to two interpretations, according to whether short-term macroeconomic equilibrium or long-term growth is under consideration. In each case, there is no necessity for the economy to be in full employment equilibrium, although this is usually interpreted to be so for long-run growth, so that the rate of investment allows a growing population to be employed. Formally, following the Harrod-Domar growth model, $n = s/v$, where n is the natural rate of growth of employment and s/v is the warranted rate of growth, v being the capital-output ratio. s/v is the rate of growth of capital stock and must equal n for full employment equilibrium in the absence of technical change. To allow for the latter, n can be allowed to include labour-augmenting technical progress. It would be as if the labour force grows faster since it becomes uniformly more productive.

From the Harrod-Domar equation

$$s_w(1 - \gamma) + s_p\gamma = nv.$$

Hence

$$\gamma = \frac{nv - s_w}{s_p - s_w} = 1 - \frac{s_p - nv}{s_p - s_w}$$

As long as $s_p > nv > s_w$, a solution exists for the distribution of income which allows the rate of saving to be brought into equality with that rate of investment necessary for full employment growing at the rate n.

The role played by long-run steady-state balanced growth is to fix a level of investment with which saving can be brought into equality. Any other method of determining the level of investment could serve this purpose equally well; for example, leaving it as an exogenously determined parameter as Kaldor does for the short run. Then $s_w(1 - \gamma) + \gamma s_p = I/Y$ where I is the level of investment. For the long-run equilibrium,

$$I/Y = (I/K) \cdot (K/Y) = nv,$$

where K is capital stock, if I/K, the rate of growth of capital, is to equal the natural rate of growth. This suggests that the conceptual content of the model is independent of its application to the short run or the long run or to some other method of fixing the level of investment. It is this conceptual content which we wish to explore rather than the applications of the model. It is important to recognise this since the model has been closely associated with the long-run application so that the distinction between its time horizon and conceptual content has tended to be lost.

The interest in the long run has been stimulated by Pasinetti's (1962) amendment of Kaldor's version.[1] Pasinetti detected what he considered to be an error in the model. Workers were saving out of wages at the rate s_w and were either receiving no profits in return for this saving or were saving out of their profit income at the rate s_p. This followed from Kaldor's saving function $s_pP + s_wW$ for which all savings out of profits were at the rate s_p whosoever owns them. For Pasinetti, workers would save out of their profits and wages at the same rate, if they were to be rational. Accordingly he proposed the following saving function in the tradition laid down by Kaldor

$$S = s_pP_p + s_w(W + P_w)$$

where P_p and P_w are capitalists' and workers' profits, respectively, so that $P = P_p + P_w$. Pasinetti is correct in his criticism in so far as the relevant economic agent undertaking saving is the individual. On the other hand, if the institutions that generate profits are also the locus of decision-making over saving, then saving out of profits is a property of these institutions and not of the individuals who own them. It might be thought that the corporate business system with retained earnings for investment justified Kaldor's approach over Pasinetti's. Kaldor's saving function places workers in a subordinate position of power in determining their savings out of profits. Nevertheless, their savings out of wages have an effect on the distribution of income, with the share of profits falling as s_w is increased. Paradoxically, whilst Pasinetti allows workers a greater independence in their saving behaviour, as we shall see, this leads to their having a minimal effect in aggregate.

Pasinetti considers a long-run equilibrium in which the stock of capital owned by each class is in proportion to the rate at which they save:

$$\frac{K_w}{K_p} = \frac{S_w}{S_p}$$

If each class is to earn an equal rate of return on capital stock owned, it follows that

$$\frac{P_w}{P_p} = \frac{K_w}{K_p} = \frac{S_w}{S_p}$$

But

$$\frac{S_w}{S_p} = \frac{s_w(W + P_w)}{s_p P_p}$$

From these equations, it is easily derived that

$$s_p P_w = s_w(W + P_w).$$

The RHS of this equation is simply workers' savings out of wages and profits. The LHS is what capitalists would save out of workers' profits if they were to receive them. Consequently, workers always save from their income what capitalists would save if they were to receive the workers' profits. In other words, the total saving made is always what capitalists would save if they received all profits and this was the only source of saving. Workers' saving, out of wages and the profits they do receive, makes up for saving that the capitalists would have made if they had received all profits.

Not surprisingly, this results in capitalists having a profound effect on the economy and workers a passive effect. Consider total profits

$$P = P_p + P_w = P_p + \frac{s_w}{s_p}(W + P_w)$$

from the last equation.
But

$$S = s_p P_p + s_w(W + P_w) = I.$$

Hence

$$P = \frac{I}{s_p}$$

This equation reveals that profits are determined by the exogenously given level of investment and the capitalists' saving rate. It is independent of the workers' savings rate and their wages. If these were higher, total profits and savings would be the same, but they would be redivided with workers taking a larger share. This brings the saving rate down to the level determined by s_p. The determining role played by the capitalists' (saving propensity) is revealed if we tie the investment level to long-run growth. Then

$$r = \frac{P}{K} = \frac{I}{Ks_p} = \frac{n}{s_p}$$

where r is the rate of profit and

$$\gamma = \frac{P}{Y} = \frac{P}{K} \cdot \frac{K}{Y} = \frac{nv}{s_p}$$

Both γ and r depend only on s_p and the exogenous parameters determining the investment rate. Now, it has been argued that for an economy to reach a state of long-run growth of the Pasinetti type it would take something of the order of eight centuries. Whilst more simple models still take a century, and so are hardly more "realistic",[2] this is beside the point if we are examining the conceptual content of the model. What this one captures is the determining role played by the capitalists' saving rate. This is the core around which the rest of the economy is built irrespective of whether it is in long-run equilibrium or not.

This is easily seen from the formula $P = I/s_p$, which is analogous to the simple Keynesian multiplier in which the level of income Y and the saving rate s have been replaced by the corresponding variables associated with profits. This form of the Keynesian system is associated with Kalecki. It gives rise to the dictum that capitalists earn what they spend and workers spend what they earn. In the case of the workers, this is the special case in which $s_w = 0$. For the capitalists the more they spend, the more profits they make, creating income out of their expenditure through the fuller employment of resources. Expenditure out of profits for consumption creates demand and hence profits for other capitalists; saving depresses profits unless it is translated automatically into investment in which case I is higher.

In this model, then, capitalist expenditure is determining whether it be for consumption or investment. Wages are purely passive. They can in principle be at any level, since they are provided for out of the work of otherwise

unemployed labour. They are not at the expense of profits
and are simply added to them to make up national income.
As already suggested, the expenditure of profits is at the core
of the economy. Having determined the size of this core,
wages and employment can be made up to the necessary
levels to permit labour to be employed to produce these
profits.

This is the extreme to which the Pasinetti model is drawn.
It can be moderated, as in the Kaldor version, by allowing
workers' saving to have an influence. One of Kalecki's (1971)
contributions was rather different. Workers would prove a
limiting factor if employment became too full. The result
would be worker indiscipline as the threat of the sack would
be eroded by alternative job opportunities and there would
also be political instability, as governments were forced to
retreat from the objective of full employment. As a result,
the amount of profits created through demand would be
limited by workers' resistance to produce them. This suggests
that the capitalist economy could be stabilised at a suffi-
ciently high level of unemployment; this represents a radical
parallel to the natural rate of unemployment in which
unemployment guarantees worker discipline rather than the
efficient slack for job search.

It has been more usual, however, to moderate the extent of
demand generated profits by consideration of limitations on
the level of investment. Within the Keynesian system, this
can be a result either of too high a level of the rate of interest
or of too high a degree of liquidity preference. Finance is too
expensive, or unavailable for investment. An alternative
explanation of low investment is taken from the Kaleckian
theory of monopoly. In pursuit of profits firms restrict
output, and hence investment, in order to maintain high
prices. Generalised to the economy as a whole, this is thought
to imply a deficiency in investment. Finally, a limitation on
investment can come from too high a level of wages. This
leads to a pessimism about profitability even if the absolute
magnitude of profits can still be expanded. This is perhaps
the reasoning underlying the arguments of Glyn and Harrison
(1980) who suggest that there is a band within whose limits
wages must lie.[3] For, if wages are too high, profitability is

threatened, but if they are too low there would be problems of generating sufficient demand.

We have presented the Kaldor-Pasinetti model as a simple version of a particular way of conceiving the economy. We have also seen the sorts of ways in which this vision may be modified. In subsequent chapters we take up these ideas in greater detail in order to expose their strengths and limitations.

NOTES

1. See Hacche (1979) for a discussion of the Kaldor-Pasinetti debate.
2. This issue is reported upon in Morishima (1973). See also Atkinson (1969).
3. For a critique of Glyn and Harrison, see Fine (1981).

7 Monopoly Demand Side Economics: An Informal Analysis

If monopoly supply side economics is built up successively from firms to industries and then to the economy as a whole, the demand side is macroeconomic in character from the outset. It is stagnationist and draws upon Keynesian notions of ineffective demand, as examined in Chapter 2. These are formulated in the tradition of Kalecki, in which aggregates in terms of wages and profits are substituted for the more traditional forms of the consumption function. In principle, the deficiency of demand arising from expenditure out of wages and profits need not depend on the monopoly structure of the economy. Monopolisation is seen, however, as an important quantitative factor limiting overall levels of demand.

Consumption out of wage revenue is limited by the level of wage rates and the level of employment. Wage rates are determined according to a distributional struggle, in which individual capitalists attempt to maintain profitability by holding wages down. In this they are aided at the aggregate level by high levels of unemployment and by the working through of the distributional effects of monopoly power. The level of employment depends on capitalists' expenditure out of profits, which is the central determinant of the economic system since it provides markets for output and legitimises, from the economic point of view, the profits that have been spent by inducing a corresponding production.

The hypothesis of stagnation depends on an increasing gap between the profits potentially available to capitalists and the actual levels of expenditure that they undertake. This growing disjuncture can be explained by an increase in profit margins accompanying a reduction in investment, since capitalist consumption is not generally considered a major influence. For, if it were, it would induce a corresponding increase in investment.

In the context of rising profit margins, Baran and Sweezy (1966) present an argument concerning the causation of crisis which centres on the "tendency for surplus to rise". Cowling formalises their views in the context of his own model. An increase in profit margins results from any increase in the degree of monopoly and this can be related to changes in e, α and H, together with overall cost cutting. For example, (i) an increase in demand with growing incomes reduces elasticities; (ii) the hypothesis of the kinked demand curve implies that firms collude to maintain α when profitability is falling, but "go it alone" in raising margins (informal collusion) when demand is buoyant; (iii) innovation and scale economies are a means of cutting wage costs and of increased concentration of firms.

To some extent these arguments have already been discussed in the context of monopoly supply side economics. The third example suggests that there is a motive for capitalist expenditure on investment. For the argument of rising surplus, whatever its validity, to have any significance for stagnation, it is necessary that investment expenditure (and consumption out of profits) be too low to sustain full employment of capital and labour.

One of the merits of Cowling's presentation of this issue is that this is explicitly and simply assumed to be so. It is stated that "profits are essentially predetermined" (Cowling (1982) p. 56) and then a number of factors determining levels of consumption and investment are considered to see whether they favour the realisation of these predetermined profits or not. The emphasis is on factors that reduce aggregate demand. What is left unexplained is the original configuration connecting supply and demand. These are predetermined profits against which any deterioration in the conditions of realisation will worsen a state of stagnation. But why does this state exist in the first place?

One reason that might be given is that profits are predetermined by the aggregate expenditure of capitalists alone so that an unemployment equilibrium in the tradition of Kalecki's macroeconomics is assumed. This has been criticised elsewhere (see Fine (1980A)) on the grounds that the whole structure of capitalist economic relations, including production and distribution, is confined to conforming to the levels set by expenditure out of profits. This is highly implausible. It would imply that any factor that increases the potential surplus, whether it be technical progress or making workers labour longer or more intensively, would throw the economy into deeper stagnation because of its confinement to predetermined levels of profits. This is Keynes' paradox of increased saving out of income reducing that income, but with profits substituted for income and the effect generalised to factors other than the effective demand-based equality between saving and investment.

What is absent from Cowling's analysis is a formal integration of the supply and demand sides to yield a determinate equilibrium. Such a procedure is undertaken by Rowthorn (1981) and Sawyer (1982). Significantly, in each case, the degree of monopoly and the level of income are taken to be more or less independent of each other with one confined to the supply side, the other to the demand side. This is unsatisfactory, although it has been common within the Kaleckian tradition. Investment increases demand but this is equally motivated by supply side competition. A more satisfactory and rigorous integration of monopoly supply with deficient demand has been undertaken by Hart (1982). In order to obtain the stagnationist result it is worth mentioning the central assumptions that he needs to adopt. These imply that "no firm has any influence on the income in its product market", without which

It becomes much harder to talk about the 'true' demand curve facing an imperfectly competitive agent since, in principle, the agent's actions have repercussions for, and hence may set off reactions from, every other agent in the economy. It is also much harder under these conditions to define an appropriate objective function for an imperfect competitor.

Hart (1982) p. 133

He also notes that the assumptions from consumer theory necessary for an equilibrium to exist are quite arbitrary. In short, Hart has revealed a true honesty about neoclassical monopoly theory; it simply cannot function plausibly, and the same conclusion must apply for its less rigorous but intimate cousin in the radical tradition of Kalecki and others.

In the absence of a determinate equilibrium, observations about the influence of changes in economic parameters concern movements around an indeterminate level of initial activity which is presumed to be in stagnation. Otherwise the method of comparative statics could be employed. Without it, for example, industries are presumed to pursue an increase in the degree of monopoly. To do this involves a decrease in capacity utilisation to deter entry. This in turn may lead to the reduction of actual below planned investment (although excess capacity may be increased by investment). Such cutbacks in investment are unforeseen by other sectors and result in multiplier effects across the economy. These are presumed to be stagnationary. Yet, to assume one sector is affected by another's change in plans is to assume it is affected by its initial plans. In the absence of a satisfactory analysis of the result of these, conclusions drawn from changes in them are highly questionable. The limitations of the analysis are revealed by Cowling's summary:

Although there are mechanisms whereby the realisation problems caused by a monopolising economy can be mitigated ... none of these adjustments is automatic and each of them contains the seeds of possible deeper crisis.

Cowling (1982) p. 67

But why is there a crisis in the first place which sows the seeds of deeper problems?

In so far as an answer is given, it depends on low levels of investment and consumption expenditure out of profits. As it is generally presumed that consumption by capitalists does increase with profits, even if at varying rates according to the form in which they are distributed, the essential problem to be explained is why investment levels are so depressed. Here a number of different and unsatisfactory arguments are brought forward which are motivated more by the supply rather than the demand side. The most important of these is that the investment function is taken to depend on the rate of profit and cost of capital and thereby reflects the benefits and penalties involved in potential investment. This restricts the motivation to invest to the rewards that are to be gained, and excludes the element of coercion associated with the need to reduce costs and defend or extend market shared in competition with other capitals. Necessarily, the approach is stagnationist. Investment is also restricted by the incentive for collusion to restrict output within an industry. This is, however, highly contingent upon the notion of given or even manipulated demand curves which are unaffected by the overall level of *income*. Here what is true for each sector taken individually is not true for the economy as a whole.[1] Because all sectors tend to stagnate or expand together, it cannot be presumed that they stagnate. In the presence of monopoly, the collusion within a sector does not preclude account being taken of the demand-induced effects of other sectors, brought about through exanding income.

At the macroeconomic level, low levels of investment have tended to be explained in almost moralistic terms. For Baran and Sweezy, given the low level of consumption of workers, investment would simply be production for production's sake and this is irrational (even for the capitalist system!) For Cowling, this argument seems to have been taken one stage further. A pure monopoly need not invest at all, and, on a global scale, investment takes place only in order to satisfy the demands of working-class consumption, however this may be determined. What is notably absent from these discussions is any consideration of the credit system. Through banking operations, any discrepancy between the predetermined levels of profits and their potential level could be made up by credit expansion. That this does not occur is indicative of an extremely passive banking sector that simply mediates between predetermined profits and depressed levels of economic activity, even though increased consumption or investment, from whatever source, would increase profits overall.

The view generally adopted in this context is that the

individual capitalist cannot breach the vicious circle of stagnation because the increase in profits for the capitalist class
would, paradoxically, be at that individual's expense. For
example, individually capitalists resist wage increases to
maintain profitability but reduce this in aggregate as a result
of demand deficiency for consumption and hence for derived
investment goods. Here is a perfect case for collusion other
than over output and price. Clearly the institutional means
exist to implement such collusion through the banking system
or by government intervention. Again, paradoxically,
working-class struggle to increase real wages, if successful,
would relieve stagnation. In this light, incomes policy to
reduce or constrain money and hence real wages appears
inexplicable. Capitalists are just incapable of getting together
to raise wages even though it would raise their profits and
moderate class struggle. They are too short-sighted and only
see an immediate reduction in individual profit.

This remains so until inflation is introduced as a problem
in conjunction with the monopolised structure of industry.
Money wage increases are passed on as price increases in
what has been termed the conflict theory of inflation.[2] This
theory has often been presented independently of the level of
the money supply. The effect of a wage increase, *ceteris
paribus*, is to reduce the rate of profit and leave prices on
average unchanged. Presumably, this will involve a reduction
of the aggregate value of μ, which will be in proportion to the
wage increase only as far it is (questionably) assumed that all
industrial monopoly pricing falls upon wage consumption.
As a result, those commodities with a relatively high element
of non-labour inputs will fall in price whilst those with a high
living labour content will rise in price.[3] If, on the other hand,
prices will not fall, and some will even rise, in order to maintain the rate of profit, it is necessary that there be an increase
in the money supply or in the velocity of circulation of
money.[4] These are not quite the same thing in circumstances
of stagnation. An increase in the velocity of circulation is
indicative of either a highly active banking sector or of
increased demand for the use of credit on the basis of
planned expenditure. Given our previous comments it is
unclear why this should not have previously resolved the

problem of unrealised profits. Otherwise, if the inflation is contingent upon an increase in the money supply, this is simply the quantity theory. It is a conflict theory of inflation only in so far as it might explain why the money supply is increased—as an (unsuccessful) attempt to moderate a distributional conflict over income, which is unnecessary since income can be increased to all recipients.[5]

The demand side of the Kalecki system has been criticised before as being dependent on underconsumptionism and consequently as more or less assuming the stagnationist hypothesis that it seeks to prove. Here we hope to have shown that these criticisms remain valid even when the demand side of the monopoly system is considered in conjunction with the supply side. In addition, the treatment of the credit system has been shown to be inadequate particularly in the light of the inflationary process and its relation to distribution.

NOTES

1. This is an example of the "fallacy of composition": what is true for an individual sector cannot be taken to be true for the economy as a whole.
2. See Rowthorn (1980) for the best account of this theory.
3. This is simply Ricardo's criticism of Smith's component theory.
4. See DeVroey (1982).
5. Orthodox theories of inflation have attempted to escape these conundrums, which arise whether posed in terms of class conflict or marginal products and utilities, by introducing self-fulfilling expectations as fuelling inflation. For a critique, see Fine (1980A).

8   Monopoly Capitalism

I. MONOPOLY CAPITALISM AS A WHOLE

In the previous chapters, we have seen that monopoly capitalism is typically studied by combining the theories of monopoly and demand associated with Kalecki. In doing so, the intention is not merely to produce an economic model but to specify a stage of development of capitalism, one which has previously characterised the United States and which is currently spreading or has spread to the rest of advanced capitalism. Necessarily, extra considerations arise which diverge from macroeconomic aggregates alone. Considerable emphasis, for example, is placed on the influence of advertising and of managerialism. We turn to consider these later. For the moment, we are concerned to emphasise that the school relies, in its periodisation of capitalism into stages, upon the use of economic variables alone. In doing so, it begs the question of what constitutes the distinction between one stage of development and another and tends to reduce other (excluded) economic and non-economic factors to epiphenomena within the framework of analysis. This is true, in Cowling for example, of state economic intervention, the nature of international economic relations and even the so-called social wage which is seen as a simple but distinct portion of the wage in general.[1] In other words, monopoly capitalism becomes defined as a state quite independently of factors such as the welfare state, the rise of multinational corporations, and forms of political representation. Possibly this is legitimate and necessary but no case has yet been made for this view. In what follows, we criticise Cowling's concept of monopoly capitalism and focus on his theory because it is well developed. His ideas are, however, to be found in other contributions.

Symptomatic of this methodological absence within his theory is the treatment of the stage of competitive capitalism.

This leads a shadowy existence in the analysis. On the supply side, we have seen that it is the ideal from which the output-restricting, price-increasing industries diverge to create surplus profits at the expense of efficiency. On the demand side, there is a parallel divergence from competitive equilibrium, only in this case it is not so much allocative inefficiency as deficient aggregate demand that marks the differences of monopoly capitalism in its divergence from competitive equilibrium. There is even reference to a competitive sector which continues to exist within the interstices of the more advanced·stage. Yet this competitive stage is never specified: neither analytically nor historically despite the important role that it plays in characterising monopoly capitalism by way of comparison.[2] It appears that the periodisation involved depends on a divergence from a model of competitive equilibrium. This is itself a theoretical construct which is far from adequate to explain any historical stage of development, such as nineteenth-century Britain, let alone able to explain any other stage by divergence from it. As it were, it is inadequate to explain the anatomy of the horse by reference to the anatomy of the unicorn. Moreover, in the economy within the Kaleckian tradition, the unicorn-like-horse of monopoly capitalism and the unicorn of perfectly competitive equilibrium unhappily rub shoulders together for the purposes of comparison.

Nevertheless, behind the whole Kaleckian school, and for Cowling in particular, lies an attempt to attach theoretical hypotheses to empirical evidence. This is not always accomplished entirely satisfactorily. For example, in considering the effect of advertising, account is taken of its potential in increasing the degree of monopoly, and a single equation is estimated to measure that potential, whilst Sturgess (1982) estimates that advertising merely redistributes demand across sectors. On the other hand, advertising is an expenditure that realises potential surplus on the demand side, quite apart from its direct or indirect effects on the degree of monopoly. This effect of advertising is heavily emphasised by Baran and Sweezy, as increasing demand and as acting as a counterweight to stagnation, but it is neglected by Cowling. Paradoxically, he gives more attention to the effect of aggregate advertising on the supply of labour, this increasing to obtain income to satisfy workers' artificially created needs.

Problems with empirical estimation arise essentially because the model of monopoly capitalism is one which rests on the interaction between supply and demand. It is difficult to assign empirical effects to the factors affecting either supply, demand or their interaction. Cowling makes no attempt to do so. That the model is one of supply and demand is itself a result of the preoccupation with exchange or market relations. It is quite explicitly recognised that his analysis is conducted independently of a consideration of the production process. In doing so, it is implicitly assumed that the stage of monopoly capitalism be characterised independently of the way in which the production process is organised and develops.[3] Cowling underestimates the significance of this question, for he appears to consider the production of labour process as in part a technical process and otherwise as a distributional conflict. Thus "the initial impetus for the innovation of the factory was *distributional rather than technological*. It was seen as an appropriate response to the lack of effort and embezzlement by the independent spinners and weavers of the putting out system" (1982) p. 91. What is important in the factory system is the denial of the workers' independence, a relation of control over their labour in the production process. To the extent that he does recognise the labour process as a relationship of conflict between capital and labour over the control of production Cowling proceeds as if this may have no effect on the technical and distributional relations which are considered to be analysable independently.

Cowling makes several references to the article by Marglin (1974). The content of Marglin's article is quite clear. What bosses do, at least at the earliest stages of capitalism, is to transform not the methods of production but the control of production on the basis of transformed economic relations in which labour-power becomes available on the market through the creation of a wage-system.[4] Labour is coerced to work harder and longer. This increases profits but not by reducing wages nor by creating increased demand. The production relations have distributional implications but they are not a distributional conflict. To be clear on this point is essential, for otherwise, when the methods of production are changing, it is even more difficult to see production relations as a source of profits irrespective of demand or of technical and distributional relations. In short, Cowling tends to see profits as the result of distributional (conflict) and technical relations alone with these relations supplemented by problems of realisation. This explains at a more general level why, for him, increases in productivity etc. may not ultimately result in higher profits. These are taken to be predetermined by the level of wages, the technical level of productivity and the level of expenditure.

The absence of production in Cowling's theory leads it to be absent from his understanding of the stage of monopoly capitalism. This has a further effect, the absence of any value theory. For Marx's theory of exploitation, the analysis of production relations in which labour is coerced to work over and beyond necessary labour time to produce wage goods is only adequately understood on the basis of the labour theory of value. This is a controversial conclusion, but even those that would reject value theory recognise the need for a theory of price determination independent of the most immediate competitive forces of the market.[5] For Cowling, however, exploitation is to be located in the market place as workers pay monopoly prices for consumption goods. It may be intended that this in some sense should supplement an exploitation to be located in production, for Cowling sees

The monopolisation of specific industries as being a long-term aim of capital allowing for the exploitation of workers via the market as well as in the process of production.

Cowling (1982) p. 11

This notion of dual exploitation is pursued no further. It begs a number of questions: that monopolisation, for example, stands against other capitalists as much as other workers unless the process is seen as a mechanical and automatic disadvantage to workers alone as consumers. Dual exploitation by market and by production is in any case problematical. For where would the distinction be drawn between the two modes of exploitation?[6] Since the overall level of exploitation must correspond to the divergence between what workers consume and what they produce, this can be divided in any proportion between exploitation in production and exploitation in exchange.[7]

This is so, however, only in so far as a value theory is absent, as in neoclassical economics. For neoclassical theory there is an alternative notion of exploitation. It is the divergence between price and margin in the appropriate market. This measures the degree of monopoly that a firm exerts in the market and it can do likewise in "production" in so far as workers are coerced to work beyond the level dictated by equality between marginal utility of leisure (disutility of work) and of consumption out of income. Here we have turned full circle in reproducing the result that Cowling's notion of exploitation depends, like his model, on the neoclassical notion of divergence from competitive equilibrium. Where Cowling does tend to break with the neoclassical paradigm is in his belief that the divergence from competitive equilibrium runs along the lines of the relations between capital and labour and is disadvantageous to the latter as the ultimate consumer in the economic process. This is not, however, a conceptual nor a necessary break as indeed is recognised by Cowling in his Chapter 5 where distributive struggle can redistribute wages within the working class and even between nations. This is a particular corollary of a more general result of the absence of a value theory in the model of monopoly capitalism. The distributional categories such as the level of wages or the level of profits are in fact *ideal* averages. There is, for example, no average rate of profit except as the simple or weighted average of those that are the result of individual industry and firm degrees of monopoly. Exactly the same applies to the level of wages. These are non-operational categories and without significance since they do not form the average around which individual rates tend to be equalised but, on the contrary, are formed as a result of these individual rates.

This extended discussion of the economic concepts of the Cowling model is of importance in its own right, but it also has two other purposes. One is to expose the conceptual limitations of the model in its understanding of economic relations such as exploitation, and to link these to other characteristics of the theory such as the absence of value and production (other than as price and supply, respectively). In the next section we show how these conceptual limitations can be remedied without sacrificing the ability to examine phenomena such as the monopolisation of markets, that is so central to the Kaleckian tradition.

A second purpose of our earlier discussion is the light that it sheds on the intellectual motivation for Cowling's understanding of managerialism, for him a most important characteristic of monopoly capitalism. Following Williamson (1964), Cowling regards "managerialism" as a distributional phenomenon. With the diffusion of share ownership and the divorce between ownership and control, managers are seen to have considerable discretion of behaviour within large corporations.[8] Cowling rejects the view that this leads to satisficing behaviour at the expense of profit maximisation. Rather the two behavioural hypothesis are taken to be mutually consistent with satisfaction being gained through the absorption of profits within the managerial hierarchy. Individually, managers have a predilection for consumption out of profits whether in the form of unnecessary support staff, large salaries or beneficial pensions and other fringe benefits. With the advent of monopolisation "management is able to siphon off a considerable proportion of the extra profits implicit in a higher degree of market control" (p. 86).[9]

Unfortunately, Cowling never specifies the range of "management" covered by this hierarchy. It might be expected to cover all salaried staff, since its remuneration is considered to form part of fixed overhead expenses.[10] In so far as there are salaried staff who are excluded from management, our remarks apply to a lesser range but remain valid in principle. What is important is that Cowling treats the relations between the strata of management as distributional, just as he treats the relationship between capital and labour. Similarly then, we observe that whilst there are distributional conflicts between managers, these are predicated upon their relationships of control over the production or other processes in which they are involved. It is only in so far as a middle management can retain some control over a necessary part of a firm's activities that it is able to participate in the consumption of profits to supplement what may already be a skilled wage. In these terms, the conflict within management is first and foremost determined by changing configurations of control as the production process is itself transformed. Here we can observe two separate and conflicting tendencies of development. With more sophisticated techniques of production and management, some tasks of control become deskilled whilst yet others are created. The conflict, prior to the one over distribution, is the one to retain the real and not simply the income status of a manager.[11] This is the light in which the formation and expansion of white-collar unionism is better understood rather than simply as reflecting the pursuit of distributional gains. The unions concerned engage in conflicts on behalf of those who are not, who are being and who have been deskilled and not simply in conflicts to raise wages or internally consumed profits.

These remarks tend to be borne out if we examine alternative views on managerial consumption. Green (1982), for example, examines the role of one "fringe benefit", occupational pension schemes, as an ideological and economic control mechanism within the market for labour power. In terms of ideological control, the schemes are an aspect of corporate welfarism, which promotes loyalty to the firm at the expense of workers' union and class allegiances. Green argues that such "benefits" are also a form of deferred wages, and so permit exploitative control through the institutionalised threat of non-, or only partial, payment. A worker who leaves before retirement age will either receive no pension at all or a much reduced one. Thus, "a permanent cost is imposed on an early leaver so that his supply wage will be reduced; at the same time costs to the employer associated with high turnover of labour-power are reduced", (Green (1982), p. 13). The use of these benefits, and others such as the company car, can be seen as a weapon by which capital can control labour. Even if we leave aside an interpretation based on the struggle over control of production rather than consumption, the evidence presented by Green suggests that fringe benefits are designed to encourage a loyal and immobile management. If upper management were more concerned to eliminate consumption of profits in the middle reaches, it would prefer to see a mobile stratum rather than one consolidating its position by lengthy occupation.

At the very least, Cowling's treatment of managerialism may be considered one-sided. This one-sidedness is related to much more fundamental and abstract deficiencies in his model of monopoly capitalism. Thus, an absence of value or production theory can be seen to lead to inadequacies in examining even the most concrete of characteristics of monopoly capitalism, such as managerialism which, like advertising, might be considered to be assigned too much significance, given what has been omitted. Before considering how the basic economic categories of monopoly capitalism might be coherently explained in the presence of both a theory of value and of production, we turn our attention to Baran and Sweezy since they have been extremely influential, particularly in the United States.

We are predominantly concerned to see how Baran and Sweezy differ from Cowling. Like him, they have a central model, which sees monopoly capitalism as stagnationist (they explicitly acknowledge their debt to Kalecki and Steindl) because of price-increasing, output-restricting monopolies. They also put aside the analysis of production relations as if these could be examined separately from and without effect on the market relations. For this reason, they do not employ the value relations associated with Marx's analysis of capitalism, but put forward the view that stagnation must be analysed in terms of an unrealised potential surplus. They confine Marx's analysis to relevance for the nineteenth-century stage of competitive capitalism alone. It is perhaps significant that Sweezy's Marxism (and understanding of monopoly) seems to have been formed whilst he was engaged in a little-known study of the Newcastle Vend; see Sweezy (1938). The Vend was a longstanding monopoly of the coal trade originating from Newcastle (see Nef: 1932). It eventually disintegrated in the 1840s with the rise of railways, which provided a source of transporting coal other than by coastal sea routes, particularly in serving the London market. In drawing upon the Vend to understand monopoly, Sweezy clearly restricts his attention to monopoly as a purely market phenomenon, one associated with the pre-monopoly stage of capitalism.

Despite their attention to the United States economy, Baran and Sweezy, like Cowling, pay little attention to the foreign sector, but argue that the excess of repatriated profits over outward investment will intensify the stagnation of the US economy. Unfortunately, at their time of writing, in the early 1960s, the US was about to move into substantial and chronic balance of payments deficit which all commentators have seen as an important aspect of the world crisis of the 1970s.

Baran and Sweezy operate with their central notion of monopoly capitalism in an interesting way. They organise all other aspects of contemporary society around it, whether economic or not. By doing so, empirical developments that contradict their outlook, most notably the postwar boom, can be used to confirm it! This is done by treating these developments as the futile attempt to overcome the contradictions and irrationalities of monopoly capitalism. Thus, advertising and military expenditure are seen as attempts to overcome demand deficiency. The same is true of state expenditure more generally. They argue that this is limited by the necessity for such expenditures to be positive for capitalism and ideologically acceptable. In other words, they must not compete with private capital, nor must they unduly benefit the working class.

Again, it should be clear that this treatment of the welfare/warfare state is simply being subsumed qualitatively and quantitatively to their notion of what it must be in order to conform to their model. As in Cowling, since there is no determination of the level at which the economy settles, the analysis of the effects of advertising or whatever might be suggestive of direction of movement but not of overall outcome. Indeed, Baran and Sweezy put forward many arguments why monopoly capitalism should be able to achieve "full employment" through demand manipulation, but they never allow this to enter their thinking, since such possibilities are dismissed as irrational and against capitalists' interests (which they are not for the class as a whole since overall profits can be increased). Interestingly, Kalecki used a similar argument about the impossibility of full employment under capitalism, not so much as irrational nor as against the ideology of capitalism, but as conducive to breakdown of labour discipline. But this was not and cannot legitimately be used as an argument for the existence of stagnation.

The discussion here highlights one further point. The model of monopoly and stagnation has rarely been developed rigorously, but it contains a supply and a demand side. Each of these is usually developed to some extent without their interaction being fully examined. This means that in looking at a particular phenomenon, such as advertising, a one-sided (supply or demand) approach is adopted. It is this that tends to create differences within the contributors to this school rather than any substantial theoretical divergencies.

II. MONOPOLY CAPITALISM: AN ALTERNATIVE

Underlying the concept of monopoly in the Kaleckian tradition is the relationship between capital and labour. From the supply side, however, the two classes are seen to confront each other indirectly. Each firm and industry exploits a monopoly only in relationship to its customers. The degree of monopoly for the economy as a whole emerges by stealth, as successive price markups are passed on to ultimate consumers who are taken to be workers. This notion has such a hold upon Cowling that, despite considering capitalist consumption as in relation to managerialism, for example, he fails to recognise that net output for the growing economy includes material costs (and investment) which belong to capitalists so that these will not, as he suggests, "come out in the aggregate wash for the closed economy" (1982) p. 34. This is valid only if there is no growth of means of production in the system, for otherwise there is a net growth of material costs and these are owned by capitalists and purchased from others at monopoly prices. This illustrates that the building-block approach to monopoly admits in principle that net monopoly is simply a distribution across all agents according to market power, and not simply one between capital and labour over the latter's consumption.

From the demand side, the two classes confront or, more exactly, meet each other as spenders. At an aggregate level, there is in fact no monopoly since both profits and wages could be increased if they were only spent. Indeed, the demand side is rarely discussed in terms of monopoly even though capital has the ability to govern the level of economic activity by its expenditure out of profits. Accordingly, as a class relation, the notion of monopoly is extremely weak within the Kaleckian tradition. This is despite its Marxist origins in the study of the relations between capital and labour, a study which in Kalecki's hands focuses on the classes in their capacities as recipients (distribution) and spenders (demand) of revenue as coordinated through exchange.

This reflects a double displacement from Marx's own approach. His analysis of capitalism is founded on the study of the relationship between capital and labour directly and as a conflict over production (rather than exchange or distribution). The class relations of production specific to the capitalist mode are ones in which the bourgeoisie monopolises the means of production (and, as a consequence rather than as a starting point, the means of consumption). Consequently, capital and labour compete as classes over the exchange of labour power as a commodity. The form of this competition in exchange concerns the level of wages, but Marx more fundamentally draws attention to the process of production. Quite independently of the level of wages, there is competition between capital and labour over the length of time, intensity, skill etc. of work. Thus, there is competition between the two classes over the production of (surplus) value as a precondition for any competition involving the distribution of commodities and income in exchange as prices, wages, profits or other forms of revenue. Quite clearly, these phenomena can be understood on the basis of a single work-place, but for Marx they are the perspective in which class relations as a totality must be observed.

This study of the relation between capital and labour in the production process occupies the vast majoriy of Volume I of *Capital* and is referred to as an analysis of capital-in-general as opposed to the analysis of many capitals in competition.[12] This distinction is important for rejecting the notion that monopoly and competition are mutually exclusive opposites. If we maintain the image of the two classes confronting each other over the production process, then the only absolute monopoly is the one that binds the two classes together. Individual capitals cannot monopolise the whole of the class of wage-labourers, although competition between capitalists is now specified as a competition to exploit labour.[13] This competition assumes many forms and mechanisms as capitalists struggle to retain a position within the configuration of economic relations. It is most immediate in the production process itself. As Marglin (1974), following Marx, demonstrates, it begins by extending the length of time of labour on the basis of unchanging methods of production.[14] At a different stage of development, it extends to a transformation of the methods of production as the factory system leads to the relative displacement of labour by machinery.[15] Paradoxically, individual capitals compete for the right to exploit labour by reducing the direct labour content of commodities.

This illustrates that the content of competition should not be confused with its mechanisms nor with its effects.[16] This is precisely the error to be found within the Kaleckian tradition. Ultimately an individual capitalist's survival depends on profitability, and this is contingent upon a great number of factors of which the direct relationship with labour is only, and not always the most important, one. Cartelisation of markets is merely one defence mechanism and it does not eliminate other forms of competition except by assumption. Consequently, phenomena such as monopolisation should not be examined from the perspective of an individual firm or industry and then aggregated to the economy as a whole. Rather, they must at the outset be related to the workings of the economic system as understood as a whole: for Marx this is by reference to the confrontation between classes over production.[17]

To a great extent these general remarks are seen to have significance when we consider what, for Marx, were the structure and processes of competition. He argues that values are formed in the first place by the process of competition between capitals within a sector. This process is the *formation of market values*. Generally, these sectoral values are formed out of the normal labour time required to produce the commodities concerned. There will be a range of more or less efficient techniques in use, each with an individual value. In the formation of market values, excess profits will accrue to those individual capitals whose individual value is below the market value.

Thus, the Marxian scheme lays out a two-stage process:

(1) Competition within sectors establishes *market values* and thereby unequal rates of profits.
(2) Competition between sectors establishes *prices of production* from those market values on the basis of equalised rates of profit.

In addition, there is a third and most complex stage of competition at which the market prices of commodities diverge from prices of production according to temporary factors affecting the supply of and demand for those commodities. It is with this third stage alone that the Kaleckian tradition tends to deal, either neglecting other forms of competition associated with the two earlier stages or reducing them to supply and demand effects.

This explains the absence of production in the Kaleckian tradition, since we are presented with given cost functions within each sector. For Marx, the normal level of productivity tends to be governed by a rising organic composition of capital, as machinery displaces labour. Capitalists compete for higher productivity by increasing the size of capital that they control, and this is highly contingent upon access to the credit system (whose effects are also absent from Cowling).

This produces a coercion to invest so that the size of normal capital within a sector rises over time.[18]

These considerations are related to the absence of value theory within the Kaleckian tradition. This absence results from the conflation of competition within and between sectors. For Cowling prices for other sectors, within an industry, are already presumed (so that cost functions and own demand function can be given). This is the basis on which competition takes place within the sector to form its own price (which for other sectors is already given). For a coherent value theory it is necessary to treat all sectors simultaneously on an equal footing and not to have price formed in all but one sector whilst this sector establishes its own price.[19] For Marx, competition within the sector establishes a normal capital and market value. This in turn is transformed into a price of production by competition between sectors as a tendency of the rate of profit to be equalised. Here again the credit system is of paramount importance as a source of intersectoral mobility.[20]

The structure and mechanism of competition detailed by Marx in this their ideal form serve as an exposure of the limitations of the Kaleckian approach. More than this, though, the analysis serves as a point of departure for analysing the conditions of monopoly capitalism that diverge from the tendential processes associated with this structure. It is significant that Marx's most explicit presentation of this structure is precisely in circumstances in which he wishes to examine the effect of divergence from the pure mechanisms of competition that it presumes. This occurs in the case of landed property where the existence of a class of landlords impedes the access of capital to the land. This results in surplus profits that can be appropriated in the form of economic rents. It is important to examine the mechanisms and effects of situations such as these.

However, this must be done with some caution. We are not after all concerned with landed property but with the various effects of monopoly. There are considerable dangers in treating monopoly or suplus profits as though they were rents, because such a procedure would conflate one set of

economic relations—those concerning landed property—
with another, those concerning the obstacles to capital
accumulation.[21] Moreover, Marx is clear that even the theory
of rent is contingent upon the historical circumstances
concerning the conditions governing the access of capital to
the land. The theory must reflect historically contingent
factors.[22]

This is equally the case for a theory of surplus profits
contingent upon monopolistic economic relations. This is not
the place to rehearse Marx's theory of rent. Suffice it to
observe that it contains within it, given its three levels of
competition and the relations between them, the possibility
of analysing those aspects of competition that concern those
within the Kaleckian tradition.[23] Differences of productivity
within a sector are understood by reference to differing individual values and the formation of market value from the
individual values. There is competition to reduce individual
value relative to market value and this is achieved through
accumulation. Competition between sectors through the flow
of capital establishes prices of production. Finally, the
divergence between market price and price of production
reflects more immediate results of the varying conditions of
supply and demand. Here we have the processes of competition (and monopoly) organised systematically in a theoretical
structure. But it goes much further than this. It also makes
clear the extremely restrictive conditions necessary for the
predominance of cartelisation and demand deficiency as well
as making clear other conditions which tend to undermine
their significance. Necessarily, the theory cannot determine
the existence or not of these conditions, since they are highly
historically specific and interact in diverse forms and with
diverse effects, as is illustrated, for example, by even a casual
consideration of the oil as opposed to the car industry, say.
It is the establishment even the examination of these conditions at a theoretical, let alone at an empirical level, which is
inadequate within Kaleckian analysis: the relative absence of
coercion to reduce costs, to compete for final demand, etc.
Further, the results of Marx's theory are firmly based on the
idea that all monopoly is necessarily partial, since any one

capitalist can only exploit a portion of the labour force and must compete with other capitalists over the share in exploitation.[24]

Indeed, Marx argues that:

> superficial considerations arise from comparing the rates of profit that are made in particular branches of business, according to whether these are subject to the regime of free competition or to monopoly. The decline in the rate of profit appears as a *result* of the increase of capital and the capitalists' subsequent calculation that a lower rate of profit will enable them to tuck away a greater mass of profit. All this is based on the complete misconception of what the general rate of profit actually is and on the crude idea that prices are determined by adding a more or less arbitrary quota of profit on to the commodity's actual value. Crude as these notions are, they are a necessary product of the upside-down way that the immanent laws of capitalist production present themselves within competition.
>
> Marx (1981), p. 332

In this context, examples of the "upside-down-way" of reality in which the laws present their appearance in competition are legion, and we close this section by listing just two by way of contrast to Cowling's conclusions. First and foremost, for Marx, monopolisation promotes the continuation of accumulation even if it may impede intensive accumulation. Rather than being stagnationary, the formation of large-scale joint stock companies is seen as countering a tendency for the rate of profit to fall and delaying crisis and recession. This is partly because such companies may accept a lower rate of profit and partly because they are able to accumulate large masses of capital.

Second, the so-called competitive sector is also seen as a source of accumulation and an important counteracting tendency to falling profitability rather than as a sector necessarily subordinated, like workers' consumption, to monopoly pricing. The monopolised sector continuously creates a reserve army of labour which is a source of low-wage, long-work labour for the competitive sector. Consequently, this sector can sustain the average and its own rate of profit and accumulation.

CONCLUSION

We conclude this chapter by examining some "policy" conclusions. In his recommendations, precisely because his economic analysis is confined to the spheres of exchange and distribution, Cowling draws on the necessity for intervening against monopoly pricing and in favour of non-inflationary reflation. Conceptually, his analysis is motivated by a sympathy with the working class as consumers, although the effects of monopoly are recognised for other strata also. Accordingly, given this outlook informed by socialist principles, he particularly recommends control of investment decisions and monopoly pricing so that "the whole system would be operated with a judicious mixture of central planning and decentralised workers' control, hopefully without either anarchy or massive bureaucracy", (1982) p. 177.

It should be recognised, however, that these policy recommendations are determined much more by Cowling's sympathies than by his analysis. A similar framework can suggest much more neutral and symmetrical policies to govern the monopolised relations between capital and labour, as suggested by Galbraith's (Galbraith and Salinger: 1981) recommendation of a CIPP, comprehensive incomes and prices policy.

We have two crucial but simple criticisms to make here. The first rests on the absence of an analysis of production (as opposed to supply) in the understanding of monopoly capitalism. In its absence, policy recommendations which direct themselves to the mechanisms of exchange and distribution are uncertain in their effects since they take no account of the continuing and determining conflict over the production process. This is why Cowling focuses, along with Galbraith, on the problems of capitalism which are remedied by appropriate economic policies, as long as these are accepted. Notably absent, despite Cowling's socialist sympathies, is any transformation in property relations to bring about the social ownership of the means of production.[25] After all, the supply and demand model essentially implies a requirement for policies merely to direct the economy back to competitive equilibrium, and as such this needs no transformation in the conditions of ownership of means of production.

The second criticism concerns Cowling's position on the relationship between politics and economics. His procedure is more or less to assume that classes have recognisable economic interests over which they struggle with more or less strength. For example, it is presumed that a loss in economic welfare tends to intensify and strengthen the working class in conflict, although historical observation might suggest that the opposite is generally nearer the truth. In any case, the approach is one in which political activity is simply governed by economic interest. Accordingly, Cowling's analysis suggests that certain policies are necessary to correct the distortions of monopoly capitalism. It is simply a question of winning the working class to these policies. Here Galbraith has the better of Cowling in so far as he analyses capitalism in terms of economic interests and a calculus of political interest groups. To illustrate our point, it could be argued that destabilising inflation is the result of working-class struggle to increase money wages, a struggle that proves futile as far as real wages are concerned since monopolised sectors pass on wage costs in the form of higher prices. Even if we accept this theory, which we do not, it cannot be argued that wage struggle should be abandoned. For it may be that struggle over wages is the principal means of organising the labour movement for purposes other than wage-bargaining. On the other hand, there may be other developed forms of organised struggle. In other words, political strategy cannot be simply read off from economic diagnosis.

The effect of these two errors within Cowling's analysis is not so serious as might be expected in current conditions, for one tends to cancel out the other.[26] The neglect of strategy drawn from the antagonisms of production is acceptable to the extent that working-class consciousness and organisation is not prepared for the social ownership of the means of production. The working class is still reacting to the failure of welfare and Keynesian social democracy by demanding that the conditions associated with these be restored. Nevertheless, we feel that the Kaleckian school, with its foundations in expenditure-based categories, neglects the importance of industrial policy, and of nationalisation in particular, and this will be an increasingly serious omission as the working class demands progress.[27]

NOTES

1. For a critique of this understanding of the social wage, see Fine and Harris (1979), where the problem of periodisation is also treated in greater depth.
2. This explains why, on the demand side, the tendency to stagnation is floundering around a central equilibrium which remains undefined.
3. For a different view see Fine and Harris (1979). For Lenin (1964); "the principal and most important feature of this stage is the employment of a system of machines for production", p. 454.
4. This interpretation of Marglin is reinforced by his most recent paper (Marglin: 1982) where control over production is interpreted in terms of monopoly of information. For both cases, the issue is not the validity of Marglin's analysis (which we believe to emphasise control to the extreme at the expense of technical change) but that it raises the question of production relations which are set aside by Cowling or interpreted as distributional relations.
5. The dispute is between those that defend and those that reconstruct Marx in the light of Sraffa. See Fine and Harris (1979) and Steedman *et al.* (1981) for a review of the issues concerned. More generally, Marx rejected the idea that exploitation can be explained in terms of distributional relations in which a given surplus is divided between capital and labour. Wages are the precondition, profits the result of the production process in which surplus labour is coerced.
6. For a debate over this issue in the context of distribution and the Sraffian system, see Savran (1979) and subsequent comments.
7. There is an affinity between this dual exploitation and theories of unequal exchange. See Emmanuel (1972) and for a critique Bettelheim (1972), Laclau (1971) and Brenner (1977).
8. The control exerted through the financial marketing (except for advertising) systems seems to be neglected by Cowling. Banks might require an interest in control, if not a controlling interest, to guarantee the security of loans. Less realistically, customers and traders may take an interest in the efficiency of their supplier, the more so, however, given the possibility of vertical integration. Cowling treats trading, and presumably banking, as merely separate branches of economic activity

that fit into the chain of monopolistic markets. This, in our view, has to be established, and is questionable.

9. This together with excess capacity to deter entry is for Cowling an important reason why monopolised firms report low profitability figures.

10. This is surely increasingly unrealistic. It must be observed that payment by salary is merely a form of payment. It can equally be made for "overhead" as for "variable" labour and is more likely to reflect a flow of wage than of profit as revenue. There is nothing in the form of payment as such which determines or indicates which it is.

11. See, for example, in Microelectronics Group (1980) the account of the development of computer programming language as being dictated by the need to control programmers rather than the efficiency of software.

12. See, in particular, Rosdolsky (1977) for the significance of this distinction in Marx's economics.

13. This view is most forcibly argued by Weeks (1982).

14. Which is the production of absolute surplus value for Marx.

15. The production of relative surplus value in Marx's theory, which entails reduction of the labour-time required to produce the bundle of wage commodities.

16. This is best illustrated in Marx's theory by the "paradox" of the expulsion of living labour. Capitalists compete by the mechanism of using machinery to displace labour relatively (and even absolutely, say in agriculture). They do so, however, to guarantee a continuing exploitation of labour.

17. This suggests that the analysis of monopoly within a partial equilibrium framework in unsatisfactory since the monopoly within the sector remains unrelated to monopoly (or competition) outside it. More generally, the notion that capitalists compete by maximising profits is vacuous since any verb (supply, demand etc) could replace compete. Competition can only be understood by reference to the economy as a whole rather than by reference to individual agents. Thus for Robbins, competition is to allocate scarce resources between alternative ends, for Keynes it is to allocate ends (supply) to scarce demands but for neither is this the motivation of individual agents.

18. It is significant that Cowling wishes to deny economies of scale at an empirical level. Part of his evidence for doing so is taken from Prais (1976) and rests on the observation that the share of the largest 100 plants has remained relatively constant whilst of the largest 100 firms has increased. This is evidence of a lack of scale economies only if there has been no finer division of labour between plants. This is highly questionable. Indeed one might expect the division of labour between plants to grow so fast *because* of scale economies that the

evidence by the criterion of plant share would suggest that scale economies do not exist. Cowling's commitment to deny scale economies may not be unrelated to the desire to show that concentration of capital is motivated by the pursuit of monopoly profits. Moreover, in so far as his model of monopoly capitalism rests conceptually on a divergence from competitive equilibrium, it is important theoretically to deny scale economies in order to allow this competitive equilibrium to exist as a point for comparison.

19. This absence of value theory has another important implication. Whilst the Kaleckian tradition sets itself the task of analysing distribution, it does so only by constructing prices *prior* to distribution, so that the latter becomes a consequence of the former as in neoclassical theory. The status of such a derivative distributional theory is questionable and contrasts not only with Marx but also with Sraffa for whom, in the classical tradition, prices are derived from distribution and not vice-versa.

20. Marx treats economic forces such as mobility between sectors, for example, only as *tendencies*. This has misled some to treat categories such as value and price of production as equilibrium concepts. Marx's theory of accumulation (and competition) quite clearly suggests otherwise.

21. Marshall, in his terminology, explicitly recognises the confusion in economic concepts produced by conflating (temporary) surplus profits with a rent by using the term quasi-rent. This terminology serves to avoid rather than to address the problems concerned. There is, in other words, no general theory of rent.

22. See Fine (1979), (1980B) and (1980C) and for an opposite view Murray (1977) and (1980). It is, of course, the conventional wisdom in economic theory since Ricardo that rent, in so far as it merits a separate theory, is determined by technology (and utility) alone. The system of landed property merely determines the recipient of rent. For a treatment of monopoly profits in the light of Marx's rent theory see Mandel (1975) and (1981) who depends heavily on the idea of surplus profits from technological lead.

23. This is so even for the redistributive effects of monopoly as against working-class consumption: "A monopoly price for certain commodities simply transfers a portion of the profit made by the other commodity producers to the commodities with the monopoly price .... If the commodity with the monopoly price is part of the workers' necessary consumption, it increases wages thereby reduces surplus-value, as long as workers continue to receive the value of their labour-power. It could press wages down below the value of labour-power, but only if they previously stood above the physical minimum. In this

case, a monopoly price is paid by a deduction from real wages (i.e. from the amount of labour) and for the profit of other capitalists". Marx (1981), p. 1001

24. It should not be presumed that capitalists simply appropriate surplus labour in proportion to the employment directly controlled. This is clear from the transformation problem. The competition to appropriate surplus labour is undertaken through a variety of mechanisms, many of which do not directly involve the use of labour (most notably, charging a monopoly price, for example). This is precisely why the basis of competition, to exploit labour, is concealed and the process of monopolisation can be considered to be at the expense of competition.

25. Although Cowling may be more motivated by immediate political expediency than an underlying belief that social ownership is unnecessary.

26. There is a famous historical precedent for this. Rosa Luxemburg's critique of militarism was based on underconsumptionism, a theoretical heresy for many Marxists. Yet her political position and insight has been highly praised.

27. These subjects are extremely controversial and reflect at a general level the relationship between policies geared towards reform and revolution. For the debate in Britain, there has been discussion in the whole of the labour movement, and even over a broader spectrum, over the content of the so-called Alternative Economic Strategy. See TUC Economic Reviews, London CSE Group (1980) and Aaronovitch (1981), for example.

9 Whither Economics?

During the course of this book, we hope to have exposed the weaknesses both of orthodox macroeconomics and what is perhaps the most popular, but still a small minority, alternative the school associated with Kalecki or the Post-Keynesians. In doing so we have engaged much of the theory on its own terms, revealed both its inconsistencies and the problems that it has been unable to deal with or which it does not even begin to confront. In our first chapter we gave an outline of what we considered the most important features of modern capitalism, stressing the role of multinationals and the breadth and depth of state economic intervention. It is the failure to deal with these developments as a central part of the economic problem that leaves economics so out of touch with economic reality, whatever its merits on its own theoretical terms. To some extent, the Kaleckians attempt to address these developments, and this is to be welcomed, but we have also examined the limitations of their approach.

In the circumstances, it is a pertinent question to ask how economics has managed to survive in this way. The crisis of the capitalist world in the 1970s placed economics in a crisis as the myths of Keynesianism became cruelly exposed. But the profession has come bouncing back through the reinvigorating debates with the monetarists over the significance of models that include rational expectations. The only rational expectation to have about these debates is that they will solve few problems in the economy, whichever side wins and whatever contribution is made to the subject of economics, as it becomes even further removed from the subject of the economy. It is important to recognise, however, that the deficiencies of economics, in terms of its being in touch with reality, are not some recent problem, brought about by the stagnation of the 1970s. When the economy is perceived to be performing well, as it has done in the past, then economists can afford to be satisfied with themselves irrespective of the extent to which they are in tune with the causes of that well-being. Recent economic realities only serve to make the long-term, and not just the short-term, drawbacks of the discipline crystal clear to all but those who, caught up in the profession as intellectuals or otherwise, continue to pursue its elusive promise of a fully-employed equilibrium with price stability.

The preceding paragraphs may be thought to reveal a strong streak of cynicism on the part of the authors, and little else. A simple example will illustrate otherwise and demonstrate the ability of economics to develop according to its own logic and customs, even when it is subject to external stimuli for the problems that it poses. In the 1960s, growth theory had begun to fade as an area of progress in mathematical economics, the latter being the intellectual pinnacle of the discipline. To some extent, a new lease of life was granted by the use of optimal process techniques associated with Pontryagin's principle. The field was once again becoming exhausted when the economy was subjected to the oil crisis.

This allowed a new set of problems to be posed. The oil crisis was understood as belonging to the economics of exhaustible resources, the building of models in which there were absolute limits on the availability of certain commodities. The fading optimal growth literature was revived to take account of the presence within the models of non-reproducible resources. The literature's organising concept was an economy in which all future markets and prices are known. Its main result was that the price of an exhaustible resource should rise over time at a rate equal to the rate of interest, as had previously been demonstrated by Hotelling (1931). Many variations of models and results subsequently emerged.[1] But what stands out most sharply is the complete insensitivity of the models to the realities of the oil sector that had been the stimulus to the economics of exhaustible resources in the first place.[2] Rather, the world of mathematical economics had fed parasitically upon the oil crisis to give itself a new lease of life. It had done little to explore the underlying economic and political causes of the crisis, except in so far as this was possible (and it was not) within the narrow confines of the existing techniques of model building.

This is one example amongst many which demonstrates what has been termed, in Marxist political theory, the "relative autonomy" of economics from the economy. There can be no guarantee that the problems taken up by the discipline and the way that they are dealt with has any firm and fixed connection with economic realities. To some extent this is concealed by the terminology employed. For example, there is a literature on the economics of nationalised industries, but it can be argued that it is a literature in name alone (Fine and O'Donnell: 1981). The debate is essentially a reproduction of the one concerning the virtues or otherwise of laissez-faire in which the nationalised industries stand as a proxy for state intervention. As a result, no understanding of the significance of state-owned property can be developed by either side in the debate.[3] But the most striking example of the insensitivity of economics to the economy is given by the revival of monetarism. As the capitalist economies of the world are plunged into crisis and stagnation, so the notions that markets clear instantaneously and unemployment is essentially voluntary, gather strength and credibility. On the other hand, the Keynesian revolution did attempt to confront the concept of involuntary unemployment apart from explanations based on wage rigidities. We have cast doubt in Chapter 2 upon the depth with which the revolution transformed both economics and economies, but this example does indicate that the response of economics to the economy is not as minimal as is suggested by the previous examples that we have given. Economics is not absolutely autonomous from the economy with no function to perform other than a mystifying and ideologically supportive role.

This makes it impossible to predict what the profession is going to come up with next. Could the theory of exhaustible resources or the tying of a new monetarism to rational expectations have been anticipated?[4] What can be expected, however, is that general equilibrium will continue to play a crucial role in the development of economics. As we shall see, its significance has grown and it continues to offer responses to the "imperfections" of the economy, however well these might be understood. For Hahn this use of general equilibrium theory is justified, not by the realities of its assumptions, but by the role it performs as an organising concept against which the realities can be judged. If the results of general equilibrium are not confirmed empirically, then there must be some divergence from the assumptions employed in the theory and these can be explored both empirically and theoretically.

This justification of general equilibrium by Hahn is open to question. It appears quite reasonable in the limited claims that it makes for the theory, by depending on further empirical investigation and by arguing the case for organising concepts. These arguments are, however, general and do not support general equilibrium theory in particular. Why not utilise some other central organising concept against which to judge the real world, other than the one which has evolved in mainstream economics? Unless general equilibrium is justified by some external reference to its own properties, Hahn is paradoxically placed in a position very similar to Friedman's, although each has derived it in a slightly different way. Whilst the latter is unconcerned to question the realism of his assumptions, preferring to rely on the empirical validity of the conclusions drawn, the former is prepared to depend upon assumptions if they give rise to an organising concept.[5] The paradox is that Hahn is vehemently critical of Friedman, since he considers that his propositions cannot be demonstrated within the world of rigorously organised concepts.

But such a world has no claim to be the centre upon which everything else should rest. This is true both theoretically and practically. For the latter, it is a considerable nuisance to attempt to understand economic events on the basis of a general equilibrium theory as reference point when this is so far removed from such events. Theoretically, it is easily shown by an analogy that the use of an organising concept does not remove the need to justify it. Consider a surgeon who is to operate on the basis of a concept of the human body which is necessarily abstract, whatever the preparatory training and X-rays. We might be happy enough with this organising concept as the basis for surgery, but be a little less so if the operation were to be performed by a vet. The vet's concept of the human body would, presumably, be organised around the notion of more general concepts of physiology. In the absence of the vet, we might find that the only available surgeon was a spiritualist who believed in the need to discover and repair the body's soul. This would be far from adequate no matter how well the spiritual concept of the body was organised. Nor would we expect the surgeon and vet to organise their thinking around the points of departure from the spiritualist. More besides, we would still prefer the concepts of the surgeon, as the basis both for understanding and action, even if these did not or could not attain the degree of conceptual rigour which might attend the deliberations of the spiritualist.

In short, the case for general equilibrium as a reference point for economics is far from established. Nevertheless, it has and will continue to offer food for thought for the profession under the illusion of bringing the analysis closer to reality. How this has been so can be understood by reference to what might be termed the informational structure of the theory. In the standard model, information is divided up into two sorts, that available to all agents—what might be termed social information—and that available only to individuals. Social information includes the available technologies and the vector of prices. Individual information covers initial endowments and preferences. Generalisations of general equilibrium theory have proceeded by changing this informational structure and have been quite inventive in doing so. There is no reason to believe that they will not continue to be inventive in the future. We consider a few examples.

The theory of the core removes the price mechanism and with it the socially available knowledge of the terms of exchange. In its place it puts the ability of agents to form coalitions. By doing so it expands the available range of equilibria and no longer depends on the fictional Walrasian auctioneer. But it only lays down the rules for coalition formation. Their use remains as fictional as the auctioneer, and the absence of the price mechanism becomes notable.

Another development has been in the consideration of expectations. These necessarily consider the path of future prices. If there are not perfect future markets, then the information about future prices passes from the realm of the social to the realm of the individual. Each agent must form subjective expectations about the movement of future prices. In this, each is placed in a comparable situation, but the same is not true for the theory of the "market for lemons", associated particularly with Akerlof (1970). Everybody wants to sell a bad second-hand car, but everybody is cautious about buying second-hand at all if it is difficult to distinguish between good and bad. In this case, there is an informational asymmetry about the quality of the goods. This may, but need not necessarily, be so in the case of screening, for which some characteristic, such as educational attainment, stands as a proxy for something else—marginal product, say (see Stiglitz: 1975). Here, the knowledge of commodities is not a perfect piece of social information. The final example to be given in our whirlwind review of developments in general equilibrium theory is of incentive compatibility. Here, individuals have an incentive to misrepresent their preferences in order to gain an advantage in the market. For example, if redundancy payments are to be made, workers have an incentive to overstate their disutility of job loss.[6]

Each of the above examples could be motivated within a partial equilibrium framework to demonstrate how the market mechanism does not work perfectly to coordinate supply and demand. The motivation in practice has been more macroeonomic in character. The idea has been to explain by these microeconomic cases how an unemployment equilibrium might be attained for the macroeconomy. This is a special case of a more general way in which macroeconomics has come to be understood. It has increasingly been perceived as a special case of general equilibrium theory in which different types of informational imperfections are incorporated. For the new monetarism, for example, the informational imperfections are reduced to the minimum by the holding of rational expectations.

But the idea of macroeconomics as a branch of general equilibrium is quite new. In the teaching of economics, general equilibrium was always thought of as the pinnacle of microeconomics. Macroeconomics was thought of as the other main branch of the subject, dealing with aggregates and, most significantly, with money. Somehow, the classical dichotomy, with its real sector of general equilibrium and its monetary sector, suggested that macro was over and above micro rather than a particular application. Even with Patinkin's (1965) exposition, on the basis of general equilibrium notions, of the invalid character of the classical dichotomy, the feeling persisted that the IS/LM Keynesianism (including a real balance effect) differed from general equilibrium.

This is, no doubt, because of the presence of the money market. But it can also be seen to amend the informational structure of the economy, since money plays the dual role of facilitating exchange in the present, whether as a neutral veil or not, and as connecting the present with the future as an asset with an abysmal rate of return but a high degree of liquidity. Not surprisingly, the money market has become the focus in the modification of the informational structure, thereby connecting it to expectations formation, initially over the future rate of interest and, subsequently, over the rate of price increase. That this could be understood within a general equilibrium context has been forcibly brought home by the reappraisal literature, in which individual optimisation is subject to quantity constraints. Here we have a new informational structure for which the ability to exchange is not guaranteed by knowledge of prevailing prices.

The purpose of the preceding paragraphs is to highlight the nature of recent developments in general equilibrium. It shows both the limited conceptual content of the theoretical novelties and yet the enormous scope for this is to continue into the future, as different modifications of the informational structure are proposed and investigated according to the tools of the profession. This is a depressing prospect and one that is not relieved by the significant efforts that have been devoted to statistical enquiry. For these have responded to the developments in general equilibrium theory with the use of more sophisticated techniques and have relied upon the availability of more powerful and common computing facilities. The result has been to yield a wealth of econometrics and associated empirical enquiry, but often little is learnt about the economy as compared to the properties of models and data sets.

To some extent, the Post-Keynesians offer an alternative. They do attempt to analyse the role of macroeconomic relations rather than of aggregated quantities; they tend to reject the use of the notion of equilibrium (although we have seen that the perfectly competitive model leads a ghostly existence within their analysis as a point of comparison), and they place great emphasis on drawing their theoretical presumptions from empirical realities. This is to be welcomed whatever the shortcomings we have managed to expose in this school of thought. The lack of interest demonstrated in the Post-Keynesian project by the mainstream of the academic profession can only be deplored, and contrasted with the popular appeal to be found amongst writers such as Galbraith. He is at most recommended as an example of an alternative, more acknowledged than pursued to further conclusions. But, if economics is to make substantial progress and break with its lack of realism, it will have to examine in its foundations the role of multinationals and the interventions of the state. For it to do so is no easier than it is urgent. The task is by no means a recipe for stale descriptive analysis. It is a challenge to be answered by the development of new theory in the light of new questions geared to economic realities. The first problem is to recognise the need for change. We hope to have argued for this, and in doing so, to have pushed off in the right direction in the way in which we have exposed the deficiencies of the existing alternatives as well as through the developments in capitalism that we explored briefly in the early chapters.

NOTES

1. For a presentation of the results of the theory of exhaustible resources, see Dagsupta and Heal (1979).

2. The best account of the economic relations governing the oil industry is to be found in Kokxhoorn (1977). See also Blair (1977) and Sampson (1975), for example.
3. A more esoteric example of the way in which economics took up an external stimulus and turned it to its own purpose is to be found in Fine (1982C), where the distinction between a royalty and a rent is found to have been a device at the turn of the century for discussing the relative merits of different types of partial equilibrium analysis.
4. Significantly, the classic article of Muth (1961) predates the new monetarism by many years, indicating that the economic and ideological conditions rather than the intellectual ones had to be ripe for its success.
5. To be fair to Hahn, he does discuss the realism of the conditions used in general equilibrium, for example, on the economic behaviour of self-interested individuals. But the major novelty in his contribution to the justification of general equilibrium theory is in terms of its role as an organising concept.
6. See Malinvaud (1977), for example.

References

Aaronovitch, S. (1981). *The Road from Thatcherism* (Lawrence and Wishart, London).

Akerlof, G. (1970) "The Market for Lemons: Quality Uncertainty and the Market Mechanism", *Quarterly Journal of Economics*.

Arestis, P. and C. Driver (1980) "Consumption Out of Different Types of Income", *Bulletin of Economic Research*.

Arrow, K.J. and F.H. Hahn (1971) *General Competitive Analysis* (Holden Day, San Francisco).

Artis, M.J. (1979). "Recent Developments in the Theory of Fiscal Policy: A Survey", in Cook and Jackson (1979).

Atkinson, A.B. (1969) "The Timescale of Economic Models: How Long is the Long Run?", *Review of Economic Studies*.

Backhaus, J. (1983) "Keynesianism in Germany", CJE Conference on Methodological Issues in Keynesian Economics, Trinity College, Cambridge.

Ball, M. (1980) "On Marx's Theory of Agricultural Rent: A Reply to Ben Fine", *Economy and Society*.

Baran, P. and P.M. Sweezy (1966) *Monopoly Capital* (Monthly Review Press, London).

Barro, R. (1974) "Are Government Bonds Net Wealth?", *Journal of Political Economy*.

Bettelheim, C. (1972) "Critique of Emmanuel" in Emmanuel (1972).

Blackaby, F. (1979) "The Economics and Politics of Demand Management", in Cook and Jackson (1979).

Blair, J. (1977) *The Control of Oil* (Macmillan, London).

Brack, J. and K. Cowling (1980) "Advertising and Hours of Work in US Manufacturing 1919-75", *Warwick Economic Research Paper*, No. 178.

Braverman, H. (1974) *Labour and Monopoly Capital: The Degradation of Work in the Twentieth Century* (Monthly Review Press, New York).

Brenner, R. (1977) "The Origins of Capitalist Development: A Critique of Neo-Smithian Marxism", *New Left Review*.

Brown, V. (1982) *Property and Values in Economic Thought: An Analysis of Scarcity in Classical and Neoclassical Thought with Special Reference to Adam Smith, David Ricardo and Walrasian Theory*, Ph.D thesis, University of London.

Brunner, K. (1968) "The Role of Money and Monetary Policy", *Federal Reserve Bank of St. Louis Review*.

Buiter, W. (1980) "The Macroeconomics of Dr. Pangloss: A Critical Survey of the New Classical Economics", *Economic Journal*.

Burton, J. (1978) "The Varieties of Monetarism and their Policy Implications", *Three Banks Review*.

Chamberlin, E.H. (1933) *The Theory of Monopolistic Competition* (Harvard University Press, Cambridge).

Clarke, R. and S. Davies (1982) "Price-cost Margins and Market Structure", *Economica*.

Clower, R.W. (1965) "The Keynesian Counterrevolution: A Theoretical Appraisal", in F. Hahn and R. Brechling (eds.), *The Theory of Interest Rates* (Institute of Economic Affairs, London).

Coddington, A.C. (1976) "Keynesian Economics: The Search for First Principles", *Journal of Economic Literature*.

Coddington, A.C. (1983) *Keynesian Economics: The Search for First Principles* (George Allen and Unwin, London).

Cook, S.T. and P.M. Jackson (1979) *Current Issues in Fiscal Policy* (Martin Robertson, Oxford).

Coutts, K., W. Godley and W. Nordhaus (1978) *Industrial Pricing in the United Kingdom* (Cambridge University Press, Cambridge).

Cowling, K. (1981) "Oligopoly, Distribution and the Rate of Profit", *The European Economic Review*.

Cowling, K. (1982) *Monopoly Capitalism* (Macmillan, London).

Cowling, K. and D.C. Mueller (1978) "The Social Costs of Monopoly Power", *Economic Journal*.

Cowling, K. and M. Waterson (1976) "Price-Cost Margins and Market Structure", *Economica*.

Dasgupta, P.S. and G.M. Heal (1979) *Economic Theory and Exhaustible Resources* (Cambridge University Press, Cambridge).

Davis, E.P. (1982) "The Consumption Function in Macroeconomic Models: A Comparative Study", *Bank of England Technical Discussion Paper*, No. 1.

Deaton, A. and J. Muellbauer (1980) *Economics and Consumer Behaviour* (Cambridge University Press, Cambridge).

DeRoover, R. (1951) "Monopoly Theory Prior to Adam Smith: A Revision", *Quarterly Journal of Economics*.

Desai, M. (1981) *Testing Monetarism* (Frances Pinter, London).

DeVroey, M. (1982) "The Double Dimension of Inflation: Money Excess and Price Rigidity, *Université Catholique de Louvain, Working Paper* No. 8203.

Diamond, P. and J. Mirrlees (1971) "Optimal Taxation and Public Production, Parts I and II", *The American Economic Review*.

Dixit, A.K. (1970) "On the Optimum Structure of Commodity Taxes", *The American Economic Review*.

Dunning, J.H. (1979) "Explaining Changing Patterns of International Production: In Defence of the Eclectic Theory", *Oxford Bulletin of Economics and Statistics*.

Dunning, J.H., K.O. Haberich and J.M. Stopford (1981) *The World Directory of Multinational Enterprises* (Macmillan Reference Books, London).

Dunning, J.H. and R.D. Pearce (1981) *The World's Largest Industrial Enterprises* (Macmillan, London).

Eichner, A.S. (1979) *A Guide to Post-Keynesian Economics* (Macmillan, London).

Elson, D. (1979) (ed.) *Value: The Representation of Labour in Capitalism* (CSE Books, London).

Emmanuel, A. (1972) *Unequal Exchange* (New Left Books, London).

Fine, B. (1979) "On Marx's Theory of Agricultural Rent", *Economy and Society*.

Fine, B. (1980A) *Economic Theory and Ideology* (Edward Arnold, London).

Fine, B. (1980B) "On Marx's Theory of Agricultural Rent": A Rejoinder", *Economy and Society*.

Fine, B. (1980C) "Marx's Theory of Agricultural Rent" in *Proceedings of the Second Bartlett Summer School*, University of London.

Fine, B. (1981) *"The British Economic Disaster*: A Review Article", *Capital and Class*.

Fine, B. (1982A) *Theories of the Capitalist Economy* (Edward Arnold, London).

Fine, B. (1982B) "Multinational Corporations, the British Economy and the Alternative Economic Strategy", *Birkbeck College Discussion Paper*, No. 111, reproduced, as revised, in Fine and Harris (1984).

Fine, B. (1982C) "Landed Property and the Distinction Between Royalty and Rent", *Land Economics*.

Fine, B. and L. Harris (1979) *Rereading 'Capital'* (Macmillan, London).

Fine, B. and L. Harris (1984) *The Peculiarities of the British Economy* (Lawrence and Wishart, London), forthcoming.

Fine, B. and K. O'Donnell (1981) "The Nationalised Industries", in D. Currie and R. Smith (eds.), *Socialist Economic Review* (London, Merlin Press), reproduced, as revised in Fine and Harris (1984).

Flemming, J. (1978) *Inflation* (Oxford University Press, Oxford).

Friedman, A.L. (1977) *Industry and Labour; The Degradation of Work in the Twentieth Century* (Macmillan, London).

Friedman, M. (1956) "The Quantity Theory of Money: a Restatement", in M. Friedman (1969) *The Optimum Quantity of Money and Other Essays* (Macmillan, London).

Friedman, M. (1957) *A Theory of the Consumption Function* (Princeton University Press, Princeton).

Friedman, M. (1968) "The Role of Monetary Policy", *American Economic Review*.

Friedman, M. and D. Meiselman (1963) "The Relative Stability of Monetary Velocity and the Investment Multiplier in the United States, 1897–1958", *Commission on Money and Credit Stabilisation Policies*.

Friedman, M. and A. Schwartz (1963) *A Monetary History of the United States 1867–1960* (Princeton University Press, Princeton).

Galbraith, J.K. (1963) *American Capitalism: The Concept of Countervailing Power* (Pelican, London).

Galbraith, J.K. and N. Salinger (1981) *Almost Everyone's Guide to Economics* (Pelican, London).

Gamble, A. and P. Walton (1976) *Capitalism in Crisis: Inflation and the State* (Macmillan, London).

Geroski, P. (1981) "An Empirical Analysis of Conjectural Variations in Oligopoly" (mimeo, University of Southampton).

Glyn, A. and J. Harrison (1980) *The British Economic Disaster* (Pluto Press, London).

Gollop, F.M. and M.J. Roberts (1979) "Firm Interdependence in Oligopolistic Markets", *Journal of Econometrics*.

Green, F. (1982) "Occupational Pension Schemes and British Capitalism" (mimeo, Kingston Polytechnic).

Grossman, S.J. (1981) "An Introduction to the Theory of Rational Expectations Under Asymmetric Information", *Review of Economic Studies*.

Hacche, G. (1979) *The Theory of Economic Growth: An Introduction* (Macmillan, London).

Hahn, F. (1971) "Professor Friedman's Views on Money", *Economica*.

Hahn, F. (1980) "Monetarism and Economic Theory", *Economica*.

Hahn, F. (1982) *Money and Inflation* (Basil Blackwell, Oxford).

Hansen, A.H. (1953) A Guide to Keynes (McGraw Hill, New York).

Harberger, A.C. (1954) "Monopoly and Resource Allocation", *American Economic Review*.

Harris, L. (1981) *Monetary Theory* (McGraw-Hill, New York).

Harris, L. (1983) "Marxist Assessments of Keynesianism Today", CJE Conference on Methodological Issues in Keynesian Economics, Trinity College, Cambridge.

Hart, O. (1982) "A Model of Imperfect Competition with Keynesian Features", *Quarterly Journal of Economics*.

Hendry, D. (1983) *Econometric Modelling: The Consumption Function in Retrospect*, Paper presented to SSRC Econometrics Conference, Warwick University.

Hesselman, L. (1983) "Trends in European Industrial Intervention", *Cambridge Journal of Economics*.

Hicks, J.R. (1937) "Mr. Keynes and the Classics: A Suggested Interpretation", *Econometrica*.

Hobson, J.A. (1938) *Imperialism: A Study* (George Allen and Unwin, London).

Hotelling, H. (1931) "The Economics of Exhaustible Resources", *Journal of Political Economy*.

Iwata, G. (1974) "Measurement of Conjectural Variations in Oligopoly", *Econometrica*.

Johnson, H.G. (1971) "The Keynesian Revolution and the Monetarist Counter Revolution", *American Economic Review*.

Johnson, H.G. (1973) *The Theory of Income Distribution* (Grays-Mills, London).

Junakar, P.N. (1972) *Investment; Theories and Evidence* (Macmillan, London).

Kaldor, N. (1956) "Alternative Theories of Distribution", *Review of Economic Studies*.

Kaldor, N. and J. Trevithick (1981) "A Keynesian Perspective on Money", *Lloyds Bank Review*.

Kalecki, M. (1971) *Dynamics of the Capitalist Economy* (Cambridge University Press, Cambridge).

Keynes, J.M. (1936) *The General Theory of Employment, Interest and Money* (Macmillan, London).

Kokxhoorn, N. (1977) *Oil and Politics: the Domestic Roots of US Expansionism in the Middle East* (Peter Lang, Frankfurt).

Laclau, E. (1971) "Feudalism and Capitalism in Latin America", *New Left Review*.

Leijonhufvud, A. (1968) *On Keynesian Economics and the Economics of Keynes* (Oxford University Press, New York).

Lenin, V.I. (1963) *Imperialism, the Highest Stage of Capitalism*, in *Selected Works in Three Volumes* (Progress Publishers, Moscow).

Lenin, V.I. (1964) *The Development of Capitalism in Russia* (Progress Publishers, Moscow).

Lerner, A.P. (1934) "The Concept of Monopoly and the Measurement of Monopoly Power", *Review of Economic Studies*.

London CSE Group (1980) *The Alternative Economic Strategy: A Response by the Labour Movement to the Economic Crisis* (CSE Books, London).

Lucas, R.E. (1972) "Econometric Testing of the Natural Rate Hypothesis", in O. Eckstein (ed.), *The Econometrics of Price Determination* (Board of Governors of Federal Reserve System, Washington).

Lucas, R.E. (1976) "Econometric Policy Evaluation: A Critique", In K. Brunner and A. Meltzer (eds.), *The Carnegie Rochester Conference on the Phillips Curve and Labour Markets*, Conference Series on Public Policy, supplement to the *Journal of Monetary Economics*.

Lucas, R.E. and L. Rapping (1969) "Real Wages, Employment and the Price Level", *Journal of Political Economy*.

Lucas, R.E. and T. Sargent (1979) "After Keynesian Macroeconomics", *Federal Reserve Bank of Minneapolis Quarterly Review*.

Lustgarten, S. (1975) "The Impact of Buyer Concentration in Manufacturing Industries", *The Review of Economics and Statistics*.

Malinvaud, E. (1977) *The Theory of Unemployment Reconsidered* (Basil Blackwell, Oxford).

Mandel, E. (1975) *Late Capitalism* (New Left Books, London).

Mandel, E. (1981) "Introduction" to *Marx*.

Marglin, S. (1974) "What do Bosses Do"? *Review of Radical Political Economy*.

Marglin, S. (1982) "Knowledge and Power", Paper presented to SSRC Conference on Economics and Work Organisation.

Marx, K. (1981) *Capital Vol. III* (Penguin, London).

Mascaro, A. and A.H. Meltzer (1983) "Long- and Short-term Interest Rates in a Risky World", *Journal of Monetary Economics*.

Mattick, P. (1978) *Economics, Politics and the Age of Inflation* (Merlin Press, London).

Microelectronics Group (1980) *Microelectronics, Capitalist Technology and the Working Class* (CSE Books, London).

Morgan, B. (1978) *Monetarists and Keynesians—Their Contribution to Monetary Theory* (Macmillan, London).

Morishima, M. (1973) "On Pasinetti and Stiglitz", *Journal of Economic Literature*.

Muellbauer, J. (1983) "Surprises in the Consumption Function", *Economic Journal Conference Papers*.

Murfin, A. (1980) "Savings Propensities from Wage and Non-Wage Income", *Warwick Economic Research Paper*, No. 174.

Murfin, A. (1982) *Monopoly and Competition: A Theoretical Reconsideration and an Empirical Application to the UK Car Industry*, PhD. thesis, University of London.

Murray, R. (1977) "Value and Theory of Rent", *Capital and Class*.

Muth, J.F. (1961) "Rational Expectations and the Theory of Price Movements", *Econometrica*.

Nef, J.U. (1932) *The Rise of the British Coal Industry*, 2 vols., (Routledge, London).

Ott, D., A. Ott and J. Yoo (1975) *Macroeconomic Theory* (McGraw-Hill, London).

Oxley, L.T. (1983) "Rational Expectations and Macroeconomic Policy: A Review Article", *Scottish Journal of Political Economy*.

Pasinetti, L.L. (1962) "Rate of Profit and Income Distribution in Relation to the Rate of Economic Growth", *Review of Economic Studies*.

Pasinetti, L.L. (1974) *Growth and Income Distribution: Essays in Economic Theory* (Cambridge University Press, Cambridge).

Patinkin, D. (1965) *Money, Interest and Prices* (Harper and Row, New York).

Patinkin, D. (1976) "The Real Balance Effect and The Neoclassical Synthesis", in M.J. Surrey (ed.), *Macroeconomic Themes* (Oxford University Press, Oxford).

Phillips, A.W. (1958) "The Relationship Between Unemployment and the Rate of Change of Money Wage Rates in the U.K. 1861-1957", *Economica*.

Pierce, D. and D. Shaw (1974) *Monetary Economics* (Butterworths, London).

Pindyck, R. and D. Rubinfeld (1976) *Econometric Models and Economic Forecasts* (McGraw-Hill Kogakusha, Tokyo).

Prais, S.J. (1976) *The Evolution of Giant Firms in Britain* (Cambridge University Press, Cambridge).

Purvis, D. (1980) "Monetarism, A Review: Review Article of Stein (1976)", *Canadian Journal of Economics*.

Reynolds, P.J. (1981) "Kalecki and the PostKeynesians: A Reinterpretation", *North Staffordshire Polytechnic Economics Department Working Paper*, No. 4.

Reynolds, P.J. (1983) "Kalecki's Degree of Monopoly", *Journal of PostKeynesian Economics*.

Robinson, J. (1933) *The Economics of Imperfect Competition* (Macmillan, London).

Robinson, J. (1973) "What Has Become of the Keynesian Revolution?", in *After Keynes* (Basil Blackwell, Oxford).

Rosdolsky, R. (1977) *The Making of Marx's Capital* (Pluto Press, London).

Rotheim, R.J. (1981) "Keynes' Monetary Theory of Value (1933)", *Journal of PostKeynesian Economics*.

Rowthorn, B. (1980) *Capitalism, Conflict and Inflation* (Lawrence and Wishart, London).

Rowthorn, B. (1981) "Demand, Real Wages and Economic Growth", *Thames Papers in Political Economy*.

Samuelson, P. and R. Solow (1960) "Analytical Aspects of Anti-Inflation Policy", *American Economic Review*.

Savran, S. (1979) "On the Theoretical Consistency of Sraffa's Economics", *Capital and Class*.

Sawyer, M.C. (1982) *Macroeconomics in Question: The Keynesian Monetarist Orthodoxies and the Kaleckian Alternative* (Wheatsheaf Books, Brighton).

Spence, A.M. (1977) "Entry, Investment and Oligopolistic Pricing," *The Bell Journal of Economics*.

Sraffa, P. (1926) "The Law of Returns under Competitive Conditions", *Economic Journal*.

Steedman, I. *et al.* (1981) *The Value Controversy* (Verso-NLB, London).

Stein, J. (1976) (ed.) *Monetarism* (North Holland, Amsterdam).

Steindl, J. (1952) *Maturity and Stagnation in American Capitalism* (Oxford University Press, Oxford).

Stiglitz, J. (1975) "Information and Economic Analysis", in

M. Parkin and A. Norbay (eds.), *Current Economic Problems* (Cambridge University Press, Cambridge).

Sturgess, B.T. (1982) "Dispelling the Myth: The Effects of Total Advertising Expenditure on Aggregate Consumption", *Journal of Advertising*.

Sugden, R. (1983) "Why Transnational Corporations?", *Warwick Economic Research Papers*, No. 222.

Sweezy, P.M. (1938) *Monopoly and Competition in the British Coal Trade, 1550–1850* (Harvard University Press, Cambridge).

Tobin, J. (1980) *Asset Accumulation and Economic Activity* (Basil Blackwell, Oxford).

Tobin, J. (1981) "The Monetarist Counter-Revolution Today—an Appraisal", *Economic Journal*.

United Nations (1983A) *Transnational Corporations in the International Automotive Industry* (UN Transnational Corporation Centre, New York).

United Nations (1983B) *Transnational Corporations in World Development, Third Report* (UN Transnational Corporation Centre, New York).

Wallis, K. (1979) *Topics in Applied Econometrics* (Basil Blackwell, Oxford).

Waterson, M. (1980) "Price-Cost Margins and Successive Market Power", *Quarterly Journal of Economics*.

Waterson, M. (1982) "Vertical Integration, Variable Proportions and Oligopoly", *The Economic Journal*.

Weeks, J. (1982) *Capital and Exploitation* (Edward Arnold, London).

Weintraub, E.R. (1979) *Microfoundations* (Cambridge University Press, Cambridge.

Wickens, M. and H. Molana (1982) "Stochastic Life Cycle Theory with Varying Interest Rates and Prices", *University of Southampton Discussion Paper*, No. 8224.

Williamson, O.E.W. (1964) *The Economics of Discretionary Behaviour: Managerial Objectives in a Theory of the Firm* (Prentice Hall, Englewood Cliffs, New Jersey).

Index